Built-In Plans & Techniques

Handyman Club Library™

Handyman Club of America
Minneapolis, Minnesota

Built-In Plans & Techniques

CREDITS

Tom Carpenter
Creative Director

Mark Johanson
Book Products Development Manager

Chris Marshall
Editor

Dan Cary
Photo Production Coordinator

Richard Steven
Project Designer, Copy Writer

Marti Naughton
Series Design, Art Direction & Production

Kim Bailey
Photographer

Jon Hegge, Rod Mechem, John Nadeau
Project Builders

Bruce Kieffer
Technical Illustrations

Brad Classon
Production Assistance

SPECIAL THANKS

Scott Rogers, Christina Dodge
Guilded Salvage, Minneapolis, MN

ISBN 1-58159-086-5

3 4 5 6 7/07 06 05 04 03

Handyman Club of America
12301 Whitewater Drive
Minnetonka, Minnesota 55343
www.handymanclub.com

Contents

Building Built-ins

A built-in is any structure that is permanently attached to your home, and therefore stays with the house rather than moving along with its residents. Successfully completing built-in furniture projects can immediately improve the daily livability of your home in several ways:

• Built-ins increase storage and/or accessibility— where clutter and chaos reign and our "stuff" seems to be taking over, a well-conceived built-in can be just the ticket to bring things under control.

• Built-ins add character and beauty. One of the most effective ways to transform an "ordinary" house into a unique and welcoming home is with beautiful, well-planned built-ins.

• Built-ins change the way a room is used. Because they're permanent, they can reroute traffic, create new options for furniture arrangements, or define areas for specialized use.

• Built-ins are also an investment. If executed tastefully, built-in cabinetry and furniture can actually help your house appreciate in value.

The most common built-in

cabinetry is found in kitchens and bathrooms. In this book, however, we focus our attention on other areas of the home and on projects that go beyond the scope of standard cabinetmaking. The difficulty level ranges from very simple to quite challenging, and you'll find a broad spectrum of materials, styles, and construction techniques represented as well. As in all Handyman Club of America project books, every chapter contains all the information you need to build a project successfully—materials list, cutting list, clear drawings, helpful photos of key construction steps, and easy-to-follow text.

IMPORTANT NOTICE

For your safety, caution and good judgment should be used when following instructions described in this book. Take into consideration your level of skill and the safety precautions related to the tools and materials shown. Neither the publisher, North American Membership Group, nor any of its affiliates can assume responsibility for any damage to property or persons as a result of the misuse of the information provided. Consult your local building department for information on permits, codes, regulations and laws that may apply to your project.

(Above) A well-planned and executed built-in project makes your home more livable and can increase its value. This 1920s-era, Arts-and-Crafts style dining room sideboard provides visual interest, lots of storage, and an auxiliary serving counter for busy holiday meals. The way it is built into the wall makes it much less imposing than a freestanding piece of the same size. People interested in buying this house know they don't need to spend more money for a dining room cabinet, and they're attracted to the charm and architectural interest that the built-in hutch creates. (Left) The companion unit to the sideboard above, this built-in bookshelf unifies the entire wall and provides even more valuable storage space. Achieving similar storage capacity with freestanding bookshelves would most likely result in the wall looking crowded and broken up; the proportions of the various elements and the transitions between them would likely be awkward rather than smooth.

A complete plan is always helpful to have when planning and building your built-in. You can always modify existing plans to suit your specific needs, but don't overlook how your changes might impact the project's structural integrity and aesthetic appeal.

Planning your built-in

There are many reasons for choosing to design and make a built-in rather than a freestanding piece of furniture or cabinetry. Perhaps you want a piece that blends architecturally with your home. Maybe your space is at a premium and you want to rely on walls for structural support. Or it could be that you want the piece to have the feel of permanence. Some built-in projects will give you the freedom of not having to retrieve fallen objects from behind or clean dust and dirt from beneath the piece.

To avoid potential pitfalls as you consider a built-in project, ask yourself the following kinds of questions:

Is the scale of the piece appropriate for the setting? Take into account the size of the room, the height of the ceiling, other furniture and how it is arranged, and how the room is most commonly used—Do people normally pass through the space or settle in? What is typical eye level of objects in the room? Will a built-in be seen close up or from a distance? Consider whether the proportions of your project will dominate a small room or disappear in a larger one.

Can I get the piece through hallways and door openings? Few experiences are more frustrating than crafting a piece in the shop and then finding it can't be coaxed around a tight corner, or through a doorway—even with the door removed. Before building large or long pieces, check the access route while you still have time to make adjustments.

Will the piece enhance the value of your home? Shoddy workmanship or ill-conceived projects don't add livability and value—they decrease it. Most of us have seen an otherwise attractive house marred by a poorly built homeowner project. Also, think twice about making a built-in cabinet with permanent shelves of nonstandard dimensions designed for a specific purpose. This is an instance where a freestanding unit might be better. Even with high craftsmanship, a built-in that doesn't suit the needs of future residents can decrease rather than increase resale value.

MODIFYING PLANS

One of the simplest and best ways to "design" a built-in is to start with a plan that's already been developed, and modify it to suit your needs. Making simple changes to existing plans can yield a truly personalized piece without requiring the time, energy, and risk that accompany designing from scratch. The projects featured in this book can be altered easily to fit your needs and space.

Changing size. Sometimes changing the size of a designed piece is simple and straightforward; other times it's not. Making an open bookcase shorter, narrower or shallower likely will involve changing only a few dimensions. However, making the same simple bookcase taller or wider might require more extensive changes. Longer shelves might need nosing to stiffen them; you may have to add a center mullion for more face frame support; materials might need to be upgraded to increase lateral strength—for example, replacing particleboard with plywood or solid lumber. In more complex cabinets, changing the basic size can have numerous ramifications. For instance, reducing

---

BUILDING PERMITS

You will not need a building permit for the projects in this book, or for most built-in projects. Whenever your project has a significant impact on mechanical systems (electrical, plumbing, HVAC) or the structural integrity of your house you should check with your local building inspector. If your built-in is going into a remodeled kitchen or bathroom, for instance, a building permit is likely required for the project. If you are replacing a load-bearing wall with a floor-to-ceiling unit that provides structural support as well as storage or display space, your building inspector will want to review it. But simply attaching a piece of furniture to your wall does not require a building permit.

Purchasing built-ins

One option for adding built-ins to your home is to purchase a unit, either used or new, modify it as needed, then install it. This approach is especially effective for getting pieces that match older homes, like dining room hutches, entry benches, or bookshelf/column room dividers. Architectural antique stores and salvage yards will often yield treasures that have been discarded in an attempt to modernize; treasures that, by virtue of their authentic materials, unique styling, period hardware and aged finish would be virtually impossible for you to replicate.

Many companies manufacture new furniture and cabinetry that is intended to be built in. Sometimes you can simplify a project (as we did with the Contemporary Basement Bar project, pages 62 to 75) by purchasing stock cabinets and using them as components in a larger project, thereby eliminating the need to make complex doors and drawers from scratch.

the proportions of a cabinet may require resizing all of the cabinet parts, including doors and drawers. When you find a design you like and you need to change the project's proportions, be sure to carefully consider all the effects of your changes before you begin building. Any modifications should not compromise structural soundness or visual proportions.

Changing materials. Generally, it's not a problem to change materials in a woodworking project. But again, there are some considerations to be aware of. Substituting one species of solid wood for another is usually no problem; each species has its own characteristics that determine resistance to wear, strength, and how it takes a stain or finish. In some applications these differences can be important, but more often they're of little practical significance. When substituting one type of plywood for another, consider availability, the visual impact of the different grain pattern, and the availability of matching wood edge tape.

Changing styling. Sometimes the style of a piece can be dramatically changed by simply switching doors. This is often the case with kitchen cabinets. Oak cabinets that are labeled "traditional" use the same cabinets as those that are labeled "contemporary," they just have different doors. You can really dress up a plain cabinet by simply substituting five-piece raised panel doors and unique door pulls. If any of the doors are on the narrow side, be sure to verify

that they are wide enough to reveal a significant portion of center panel in addition to the necessary stiles (usually at least 7 in. for flat panels and 8 in. for raised panels).

Modifying with molding. Another way to change the styling of a piece is with molding—by deleting it, adding it or changing it. Moldings are available in a wide range of profiles, from understated to ornate. Molding manufacturers often can provide suggestions for ways to combine stock moldings for creative effects.

SAFETY TIPS

· Wall-mounted built-ins must be securely installed and attached: there is no harm in overkill. Needs and usages change, so always fasten units directly to studs. And make sure there is either a sturdy hang strip or the cabinet back is capable of supporting the weight.

· It is illegal and dangerous to permanently cover an electrical junction box. If your built-in cabinet covers an electrical outlet or switch, you need to provide access (usually a hole cut in the cabinet back) to the junction box unless you eliminate the junction by pulling new wires through to the relocated receptacle or switch.

Making a cardboard prototype is an inexpensive way to eliminate proportional surprises you may encounter once the built-in is installed. If the prototype looks too large or small in the room, make adjustments to correct the scale.

Outline the project area with tape to make sure it fits with the rest of the room. Pay particular attention to traffic paths and door swing clearances. For floor-to-ceiling projects, create tape outlines on the ceiling as well to make sure you're clear of lights, cabinets or other obstructions.

OTHER FACTORS TO CONSIDER WHEN DESIGNING A BUILT-IN

Function. What do you want the piece to do? Is its purpose mostly practical—for example, efficient storage? Or is it mostly visual, such as false beams on a ceiling? Function can be aesthetic as well as practical, but identifying the desired function is the first step to a good design. Projects that need to accommodate standardized components like electronics or appliances will require precise shelf and cabinet opening dimensions. In contrast, bookshelves with adjustable shelving are more dimensionally flexible without compromising function in the least.

Proportion. The perception of project size can be influenced by how the project is finished, especially if a color is involved. A cabinet that blends in with its setting will intrude less upon a space than one finished with a bright coat of paint, and a light-colored piece usually will appear smaller than a dark one. Thus, if your project will be quite large, consider using light-toned wood, like birch or maple, or painting it off-white.

Style. Do you want the piece to blend seamlessly into its setting? Or do you want it to contrast lively with surrounding woodwork and furnishings? Either approach can work well, but you should consider the architectural character of your house. If you live in a Craftsman-style bungalow and you want your built-in bookshelf to look as if it has always

been there, you'll build it of quarter-sawn oak with a medium stain, not white melamine.

THE DESIGN PROCESS

It's easier and cheaper to fix mistakes or make modifications on paper than halfway through the construction or installation process. Thus, even if you're sure you can visualize exactly how the project will look and how it will go together, we recommend making scaled drawings—or at least sketches with measurements—to work through all the details before you start cutting and assembling. Scaled drawings are especially helpful in making decisions about proportions of the various elements, which can have a significant impact on the overall look and success of the piece. Clumsy or awkward proportions cannot be corrected with craftsmanship.

Visualization. It is very helpful to be able to accurately visualize the impact of your specific piece in its setting before you build it. There are a couple of devices you can use to help in this regard.

Mock-ups. Constructing a mock-up is one of the best ways to know for sure how the project will fit into the room proportionally. The mock-up needn't look like the proposed project. You can simply lay out the project footprint on the floor with masking tape or newspapers. Or you can pile up chairs or boxes to approximate the size and shape.

Hanging strings or tape from the ceiling can point out potential scale issues in floor-to-ceiling projects. Whichever method you use, live with the mock-up for a while before making up your mind.

Drawings. Create a scale drawing of the entire room, including architectural features like windows and doors, as well as the room furnishings. Draw or make a scaled cutout of the planned project and position it on the scaled drawing. Evaluate how well it fits and try moving it or changing the size.

Site evaluation. Carefully review the installation site before you begin to build. Site conditions might warrant design modifications. If, for instance, the size of your planned bookshelf interferes with an existing light switch, you might decide to make the piece a few inches smaller rather than move the switch.

Check the walls for straightness and to see if they're plumb. Check that the floor is level, both parallel to the wall at the depth of the finished cabinet and perpendicular to the wall at several points. If the built-in piece is being installed in a corner, check the corner for square. Most of the projects in this book have extended sides and toekicks designed to provide ½ to ¾ in. of scribing space for accommodating site conditions that vary from level, plumb, and square. If you find variations significantly greater than this amount, you might want to modify the design by increasing the scribe, or plan on using applied moldings, like base shoe or quarter-round, to achieve a tight fit.

Review the plan. Read through the plan completely before you start. Do you have all the tools you need? Are you comfortable executing the techniques called for? If the plans include written construction steps (as in this book) do you understand them? If written steps are not included, plan your own logical sequence. Also review the materials and supplies needed. What do you have on hand, what do you need to buy? Will you use all the materials as specified, or are you making some modifications? Review all the ramifications of any changes you plan to make—for example, if you want to change to a different wood species, is it available in the sizes called for? Is matching edge tape available if needed? Does it mean you'll want to use a different finish? Revise the cutting list as needed and assemble all materials and supplies.

Make cutting diagrams for any sheet goods used in the project. This is especially important with plywood, when not only the size but the grain direction matters. It is also valuable with lumber and moldings, when you often need to cut a variety of shorter pieces from a few long pieces. Taking the time to organize and prepare before you start will help you reduce waste and make economical use of both time and materials.

Check actual measurements. Confirm measurements and

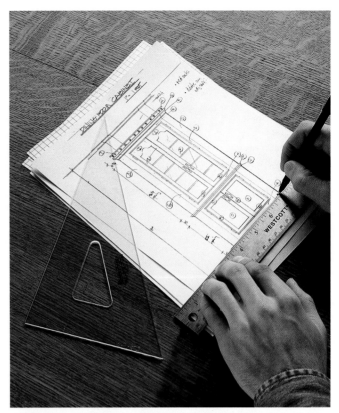

Make scaled drawings of your built-in project to determine pleasing proportions and to help you assess how well the built-in will fill the space. Use the drawing as a reference when cutting parts and assembling the built-in.

cut pieces as you go. Do not cut all the pieces on the cutting list at once with the idea of assembling them like a kit. Confirming actual measurements before cutting enables you to make on-the-spot adjustments when slight discrepancies occur (as they typically will), and it prevents minor problems from compounding into major ones.

SITE PREPARATION

Unlike freestanding furniture, you can't just tote your newly finished built-in into the room and set it in place. Because you're anchoring it permanently in the room, the site should be prepared.

Moldings. Carefully remove the baseboard and ceiling cove moldings, setting them aside for trimming and reinstallation.

Carpet. Pull back the carpet for the most solid installation; cut to size, restretch, and reinstall after installation. If you decide to simply install the built-in on top of existing carpet, make sure the piece is level, stable, and well shimmed so that no further settling will occur due to carpet compression.

Mechanicals. Deal with any mechanical issues; move switches or outlets, measure for access openings in cabinets, reroute or extend heat ducts or cold-air returns. Hire professionals for these tasks if you're not comfortable doing

Check walls for plumb in several spots within the proposed installation area. Use a 3- or 4-ft.-long carpenter's level or suspend a plumb bob from the ceiling and measure the distance from the string to the wall at several points.

Check floors for level at the proposed built-in site, using a 3- or 4-ft.-long carpenter's level.

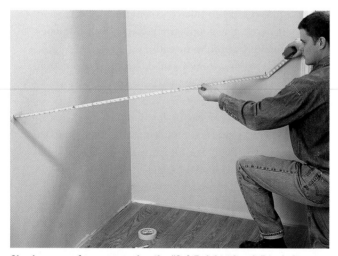

Check corners for square using the "3-4-5 right triangle" technique or by snapping perpendicular chalklines.

them yourself, and make sure to follow applicable permit and inspection practices.

Studs. Locate and mark the wall studs. If appropriate, add any furring strips or cross pieces needed for a secure installation.

THE INSTALLATION PROCESS

With any built-in project, it's important to establish a strategy for installing the project parts. In general, start with the corner cabinet, the base cabinet or the "anchor" cabinet if your project includes cabinetry. Position it, using shims, at the floor and the wall. Scribe as needed (See page 15). Fasten the cabinets to the wall with drywall screws. Attach other pieces to the cabinet, wall and floor.

Doors. The best time to mount doors is during the assembly process while you're working in your shop. Then, remove the doors for finishing and installing the unit. Reinstall the doors and make final hinge adjustments after installing the cabinet boxes.

Finishing. The two finishing issues critical to built-in projects are when to apply the finish and how best to match existing woodwork. Built-in projects can be finished either in the shop or on site. Both strategies have merit, and neither is the best in every situation. Generally speaking, projects that are virtually completed in the shop and then transported to the installation site are best finished in the shop. Applying the finish in the shop gives you more convenient access to the parts, it allows you to finish broad vertical surfaces while they are horizontal (reducing the possibility of sags and runs), and it protects the installation site from damage or spills. Conversely, projects that are built principally at the installation site are usually best finished after installation is complete, allowing the pieces to be trimmed, fitted, fastened and sanded while the wood is raw.

A third option combines the best of both the preceding approaches: partially finish the project in the shop, then complete the finishing on site. In this case the stain or primer (sometimes even the first topcoat) is applied in the shop where conditions are more controlled and flexible, with final topcoating and touch-up done after installation. This approach reduces much of the risk and mess at the site, yet you can still apply the final finish after the transporting, fitting and fastening steps have been done.

Matching the finish on existing woodwork in an older home is more art than science. It involves keen observation, a sharp eye for nuance and lots of patience. A number of factors combine to make your existing finish what it is— cut and color of the original wood; the composition of any stain used and how deeply it penetrated; the color, thickness and sheen of the topcoat; and the effects of natural wood aging and patina on each of these variables.

Top treatments for built-ins

Option 1: Build a soffit to help integrate the built-in with the house. Soffits can be partial, to flatten a corner as shown, or they can cover the full depth of the built-in.

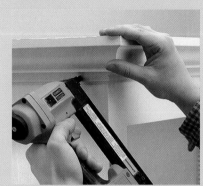

Option 2: Stop short of the ceiling and attach crown molding to the top of the project. Leaving open space at the top can make the built-in seem less massive, and it allows more design flexibility.

Option 3: Build all the way from floor to ceiling; then conceal the joint at the top with crown or cove molding, blending the molding in with any existing ceiling trim.

Remove trim molding in the proposed project area before beginning the installation. Removing the trim allows you to inspect the wall/floor joint and can provide information about the trim finish. It also provides flat access to the wall for a clean installation.

To match the original stain color, experiment on new wood with ready-mixed stains and, if necessary, combinations of stains, until you achieve a satisfactory color match. To match the topcoat, you don't necessarily have to use the same product as the original (after all, it won't look the same when newly applied as it will after years of aging anyway); your goal is to make it look the same. Most woodwork before 1930 was finished with shellac. Then varnish became the preferred finish, and within the last couple of decades polyurethane has become the predominant topcoat. Whatever the original topcoat, you can most likely achieve an acceptable match using polyurethane by manipulating the three variables of color, thickness and sheen. Color can be changed by adding pigment to tint the polyurethane. Polyurethane is available in a range of

sheens, from very flat matte to satin to slick high-gloss. Thickness depends on the number of coats applied. Remember, when applying multiple coats, to let each coat completely dry (follow the instructions on the container) before applying the next. Experiment on wood scraps until you achieve a match.

The most challenging situation for finish-matching is when two pieces touch each other. The point where new and old meet is where the eye will most easily notice any discrepancies that still exist after you've done your best to achieve a match. If you're installing a piece where newly finished wood abuts or overlaps old, and a noticeable discrepancy still exists, one solution is to replace a portion of the existing woodwork with new. In such cases, you might want to consider replacing all the baseboard in the room, yet leaving the existing door casing and window frame. The fact that they are separated from the new woodwork by wall space makes it less likely that the eye will notice minor differences in finish.

Plywood is manufactured in several thicknesses, using a variety of wood species to create the core, but ¾-in.-thick laminated veneer-core plywood with smooth hardwood veneer faces is the type used most frequently for built-in projects.

Medium-density fiberboard (MDF) is growing in popularity as a veneer substrate, paintable surface, and as a raw material for moldings.

Particleboard is used almost exclusively as a substrate for plastic laminate or veneer, especially for countertops. It is inexpensive but lacks sufficient strength to be used for shelving or structural members.

Melamine board is faced at the factory with melamine laminate. The thermofusing process used to apply the melamine creates a much stronger bond than you can achieve with plastic laminate applied at the worksite.

Sheet Goods

The basic structural component of most built-ins is some form of sheet stock; most frequently plywood. Other commonly used sheet goods are particleboard, fiberboard, melamine panels and hardboard.

Plywood. Plywood is fashioned from sheets of wood veneer, primarily pine and fir. By orienting the wood grain of each laminated sheet so adjacent sheets are perpendicular, the product is able to withstand greater stress than construction lumber of the same thickness. In addition, it is more dimensionally stable. Grades of plywood with hardwood face veneer and a range of core options are a favored material for constructing built-ins.

Most lumberyards stock furniture-grade plywood in several thicknesses and face veneer options (pine, red oak, birch and maple are the most common face veneers). Lumberyards and wood products distributors carry or can order plywood with dozens of additional veneer options.

Selecting plywood. Choosing the right plywood for your built-in project is an important task. In addition to the various core, thickness and face veneer options, you'll also need to make a decision on the plywood *grade.* Basically, there are two grading systems in use today. The one most people are familiar with is administered by the *APA (Engineered Wood Association,* formerly the *American Plywood Association).* The *APA* grade stamps (See Illustration, next page) are found on sanded plywood, sheathing and structural (called *performance-rated*) panels. Along with grading each face of the plywood by letter (*A* to *D*) or purpose, the *APA* performance-rated stamp lists other

NOTICE

Particleboard and MDF usually contain urea formaldehyde resins that continue to emit low levels of formaldehyde gas for at least six months as they cure. People with high sensitivity to chemical vapors should limit the number of composite panels added to a room at one time. Always wear a particle mask or respirator as required and provide adequate dust collection and ventilation when cutting or shaping these products.

information such as exposure rating, maximum allowable span, type of wood used to make the plies and the identification number of the mill where the panel was manufactured. Many hardwood-veneer sanded plywood panels are graded by the *Hardwood Plywood and Veneer Association (HPVA)*. The *HPVA* grading numbers are similar to those employed by *APA:* they refer to a *face grade* (from A to E) and a *back grade* (from 1 to 4). Thus, a sheet of plywood that has a premium face (A) and a so-so back (3) would be referred to as *A-3* by *HPVA* (and *AC* by *APA*).

Particleboard. Particleboard possesses several unique qualities that might make it a good choice for your next built-in project—particularly if the project includes a counter or tabletop. Particleboard is very dimensionally stable (it isn't likely to expand, contract or warp); it has a relatively smooth surface that provides a suitable substrate for laminate; it comes in a very wide range of thicknesses and panel dimensions; and it is inexpensive. But particleboard does have some drawbacks: it lacks stiffness and shear strength; it has poor screw-holding ability; it degrades when exposed to moisture; it's too coarse in the core to be shaped effectively; and it's heavy.

MDF. Medium-density fiberboard (MDF) is similar to particleboard in constitution, but is denser and heavier. The smoothness and density of MDF make it a good substrate choice for veneered projects: the rougher surface of particleboard and most plywoods do not bond as cleanly with thin wood veneer. You can even laminate layers of MDF to create structural components that can be veneered or painted. MDF is also increasing in popularity as a trim molding material.

Melamine board. Melamine is fashioned with a particleboard core with one or two plastic laminate faces. Thicknesses range from ¼ to ¾ in. Stock colors at most lumberyards and building centers generally are limited to white, gray, almond and sometimes black. Other colors may be available through special order. The panels are oversized by 1 in. in each dimension (a 4 × 8 sheet is actually 49 × 97 in.) because the brittle melamine has a tendency to chip at the edges during transport. Plan on trimming fresh edges.

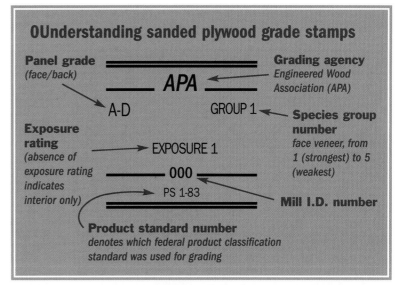

Every sheet of plywood is stamped with grading information. On lower-grade panels, such as exterior sheathing, the stamp can be found in multiple locations on both faces. Panels with one better-grade face are stamped only on the back, and panels with two better-grade faces are stamped on the edges.

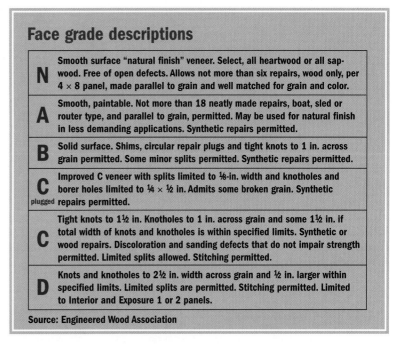

Face grade descriptions

N	Smooth surface "natural finish" veneer. Select, all heartwood or all sapwood. Free of open defects. Allows not more than six repairs, wood only, per 4 × 8 panel, made parallel to grain and well matched for grain and color.
A	Smooth, paintable. Not more than 18 neatly made repairs, boat, sled or router type, and parallel to grain, permitted. May be used for natural finish in less demanding applications. Synthetic repairs permitted.
B	Solid surface. Shims, circular repair plugs and tight knots to 1 in. across grain permitted. Some minor splits permitted. Synthetic repairs permitted.
C plugged	Improved C veneer with splits limited to ⅛-in. width and knotholes and borer holes limited to ¼ × ½ in. Admits some broken grain. Synthetic repairs permitted.
C	Tight knots to 1½ in. Knotholes to 1 in. across grain and some 1½ in. if total width of knots and knotholes is within specified limits. Synthetic or wood repairs. Discoloration and sanding defects that do not impair strength permitted. Limited splits allowed. Stitching permitted.
D	Knots and knotholes to 2½ in. width across grain and ½ in. larger within specified limits. Limited splits are permitted. Stitching permitted. Limited to Interior and Exposure 1 or 2 panels.

Source: Engineered Wood Association

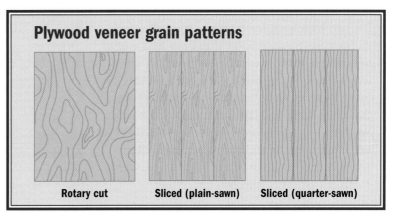

Plywood veneer grain patterns

Rotary cut   **Sliced (plain-sawn)**   **Sliced (quarter-sawn)**

1 Test-fit the carcase side, front and back panels by fitting and clamping them together. Adjust the parts as needed to achieve square corners and flush joints.

2 Apply wood glue to the edges of the parts, then clamp the parts together to form the carcase. Wood cauls (straight strips of scrap wood) distribute the clamp pressure evenly.

3 Test the carcase to see if it's square, using a framing square or by measuring diagonally from opposing corners. When the diagonal measurements are equal, the carcase is square and you can go ahead and reinforce the joints with wood screws.

Tip: *Adjust the carcase by applying a bar clamp or pipe clamp along one of the diagonals. Tightening the clamp will cause the carcase to "rack" slightly in the direction of pressure. You can also push or pull on the clamp heads to make adjustments.*

Making face frames

Many built-in projects are designed with a face frame that's mounted to the front opening of the cabinet box. The face frame conceals the front edges of the box, provides bearing surfaces for hinges and adds a bit of structural support. Some are even dressed up with decorative flutes or edge profiling. Generally, the rails (horizontal members) and stiles (vertical members) of a face frame are butted together, not mitered. The stiles are allowed to run the entire height of the built-in cabinet, with the ends of the rails butted against them. Glue and dowels, pocket screws, biscuits or splines are normally used to reinforce face frame joints.

Face frames are built independently from the built-in cabinet carcase so they can be squared up accurately before they're mounted.

How to scribe attached side panels

Few rooms are truly square. Installing built-ins usually requires that you make adjustments to the built-in so it can be structurally square but still fit neatly into the room. In some cases you can caulk gaps or cover them with trim moldings. But if you want your project sides to nestle snugly up against the walls, *scribing* is a better solution.

Scribing involves tracing the contour of the wall surface onto the outer side panel of your built-in project with a compass, then trimming the panel so the scribed edge follows the wall's contour. Most frequently, scribing is done to side panels, since the tops and bottoms typically are treated with base or crown molding. The panels can be scribed and trimmed before or after they are attached to the built-in, provided the original panel is sized with a scribing overhang, as most of the projects in this book are.

1 NOTE: *The side panel in the photos above was deliberately sized with a slight overhang at the back to allow for scribing.* With the built-in unit level, plumb and in position (but not installed), set the legs of a compass so the distance between them equals the widest gap between the panel and the wall.

2 Orient the compass so the marking leg is away from the wall, then trace the wall contour onto the panel. Mark the side panel, then pull the unit away from the wall and trim the back edges along the contour lines. For minor adjustments, use a belt sander to remove waste; for longer cuts, use a jig saw.

How to scribe an unattached side panel (also called a finished end)

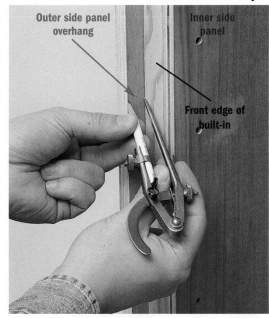

Outer side panel overhang

Inner side panel

Front edge of built-in

1 Clamp the oversized side panel to the side of the built-in. The back edge of the panel should contact the wall at its furthest point of projection. The front edge of the panel should be parallel to the front edge of the built-in. Set the legs of a compass to equal the amount that the side panel overhangs the front of the built-in.

2 With the outer side panel clamped in the same position, trace the wall contour onto the outer face of the panel along the back edge, keeping the non-marking leg of the compass in constant contact with the wall.

3 Remove the panel and cut along the contour line with a saw or belt sander. Test the fit. The front edge should be flush with the rest of the built-in, and the back edge should butt evenly against the wall. Fine-tune the scribe cut as needed, then attach the outer side panel to the built-in.

Basic Skills: Installing shelves

Many built-in projects built from sheet goods contain shelving. Because the edges of most sheet good products are not meant to be left exposed, some type of shelf edge treatment is desirable. There are a number of ways to neatly and simply conceal the edges of shelving (See photo, left). When choosing which method to use, consider the complex-

(A) Solid-wood shelf-edge can be purchased ready-made in a variety of sizes, wood species and profiles. Or, you can cut your own by shaping the edge of a board and ripping it to width on your table saw (See sequence, below).

(B) Iron-on edge tape made from matching wood veneer is a convenient, economical and attractive product for treating shelf edges.

(C) Exposed edge. For some types of projects made with higher-grade plywood (such as apple ply or Baltic birch), leaving the shelf edge untreated can be an effective design feature.

(D) Filled and painted. If you're planning to paint your woodworking project, you can simply fill any voids or imperfections in the shelf edge with wood putty or even joint compound, then sand the edge smooth before painting.

(E) Plastic T-slot shelf edge trim can be used to cover the exposed edges of shelving. Available at most woodworking or cabinet supply stores, it fits into a T-slot in the edge (the slot can be cut with a router or your table saw). T-slot trim has definite commercial characteristics and the color selection is usually limited to white, black or brown.

How to make custom shelf-edge

1 Choose a board that's the same thickness as the shelving material and the same species as the face veneer. Mount an edge-forming bit into your router table (a single or double Roman ogee bit is a good choice) and shape the edge of the board.

2 Rip-cut the shelf edge from the board on your table saw. If your shelving is ¾ in. thick, rip the shelf-edge so it's ¾ × ¾ in. To make more shelf-edging, shape the freshly cut edge, then rip to width again.

ity, the cost and how well each type will meet your design standards. Make this decision up front, since it can have an effect on the dimensions of your project (if you are using solid shelf-edge, for example, you'll normally want to reduce the width of your shelving by ¾ in.).

The other shelving decision you'll need to make is choosing a method for supporting the shelves, particularly any adjustable shelves you may be building into the project design. A common practice when designing larger casework, like bookcases and entertainment centers, is to glue a fixed shelf (usually a middle shelf) into dadoes in the cabinet side, then install adjustable shelves above and below. The adjustable shelves typically employ pins or another type of shelf hardware. When designing your project, calculate your likely adjustable shelf heights so you can keep guide holes to a minimum.

Options for supporting shelves

Dado grooves cut to the thickness of the shelves (¾ in. wide, typically) can be cut up to halfway through the thickness of the cabinet side or shelf standard (⅜ in. for ¾-in. stock). The dado provides a very sturdy bed for the shelf, especially when reinforced with glue and finish nails. But if the fit is too tight or the wood moves, bowing or breaking of the joint can occur. A dado is used only for the fixed shelf or shelves.

Shelf standards recessed into grooves in the cabinet side can be connected mechanically to shelf support tabs. This type of system provides strong support and plenty of shelf positioning options. The main drawback is their appearance: in most cases, the brackets will be visible when viewing your project from the front. Cutting the grooves also takes a little patience, and getting the slots in the brackets to line up can be tricky.

Shelf shown in cut-away

Shelf pins are made in many sizes, styles and materials. The brass pins with mating grommets shown above are on the higher end of the shelf-pin spectrum. The grommet prevents the weight of the shelf from causing the support pin to ream out the guide hole. Use a piece of perforated hardboard as a drilling guide for locating guide holes.

Shelf shown in cut-away

Dowel pins are very economical to use. The photo above shows fluted, ¼-in.-dia. dowel pins. You can make your own pins simply by cutting doweling to length (be sure to use hardwood doweling, however). If you rest the shelf directly on the dowel pins, it can roll, so cut dowel recesses in the shelf ends with a router and straight bit.

Shelf shown in cut-away

Plastic clips are inexpensive and reasonably sturdy. They're inserted into guide holes like those drilled for shelf pins, but the shape of the clips transmits part of the shelf load onto the cabinet sides.

Side-mounted drawer glides are installed in cabinets and casework that does not have a face frame.

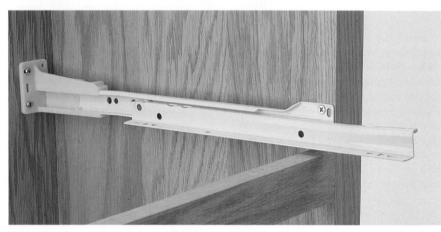

Rear/front-mounted drawer glides are installed in cabinets and casework that does have a face frame. The rear mounting bracket is sold as an accessory for most side-mounted glides.

Mounting drawers and cabinet doors is one of the last steps in a built-in project.

When it comes to hanging drawers, you can spend a lot of time building custom wood slides and glides, or you can purchase metal drawer slides that are sized to match the drawers and drawer openings in your project. By the same token, you can use a combination of traditional butt hinges and latches to hang doors on your cabinetry project; or you may prefer to try some of the contemporary and European self-closing hinges that most cabinetmakers have come to depend upon. These newer products are usually easier to install and almost always easier to adjust, eliminating most of the headaches associated with hanging cabinet doors and drawers.

As a rule, decide which kind of hinges, slides and hangers you'll be using before you finalize your project design.

How to hang a drawer using metal slides

1 Mount the inner half of each drawer glide assembly to a drawer side. Follow the manufacturer's instructions for spacing. With some hardware, you may need to trim the back end to fit.

2 Mount the outer half of the glide mechanism to the inside of the cabinet, according to the manufacturer's directions for spacing. Most drawer glides have adjustable screw holes so you can locate the glide precisely where you want, after testing the fit by inserting the drawer into the drawer opening.

Basic Skills: Applying plastic laminate

Durable, inexpensive and available in many dozens of colors and styles, plastic laminate is a building product you should get to know. Used most frequently as a countertop or tabletop surface, it also can be applied to drawer fronts, cabinet doors, or even inside cabinets and drawers where a moisture-resistant, easy-to-clean surface is desirable.

Plastic laminate is sold in standard widths of 24, 36, 48 and 60 in. at building centers (or, simply look in your telephone book under the *Countertops* listing). You can order it in other sizes or even have it laminated onto a custom-sized substrate.

Particleboard and MDF are the two most common substrates for applying plastic laminate. Both have smooth surfaces that accept contact cement well. They are also very stable. But if your project will be exposed to constant moisture, use sanded, exterior-grade plywood for the substrate.

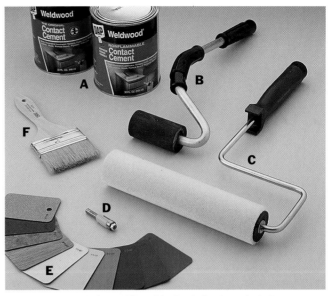

Tools and materials for working with plastic laminate include: (A) Contact cement to bond laminate to substrate (use nonflammable product if working indoors or in an enclosed area); (B) J-roller; (C) paint roller with short-nap adhesive sleeve; (D) Flush-cutting, piloted router bit; (E) Sample chips for making product selection; (F) Disposable paintbrush for applying cement in tight areas.

How to apply plastic laminate

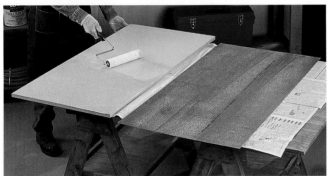

1 The laminate sheet should overhang the edges of the substrate by ½ to 1 in. on all sides. Working on a flat, smooth surface, use a paint roller with a short-nap adhesive sleeve to roll a thin, even coat of contact cement onto the top surface of the substrate and the back face of the laminate.

2 To prevent the two cemented surfaces from bonding together while you position the laminate sheet, insert thin wood spacers at 6 in. intervals between the laminate and the substrate. Once the laminate sheet is positioned correctly, remove the spacers one at a time, starting at one end and working in order to the other end.

3 Use a J-roller to roll the laminate. Rolling creates a strong bond between the laminate and the substrate. Start in the middle of the workpiece and work toward the edges, rolling the J-roller in one direction only (this allows any trapped air bubbles to escape).

4 Trim off the excess laminate so the edge is flush with the substrate. For best results, use a router or laminate trimmer with a piloted, flush cutting bit. Smooth out any roughness from the router using a fine file.

Fill nail and screw holes, voids in plywood edges, and other surface defects with paintable or stainable wood putty. Overfill the area slightly, allow the putty to dry, then sand the putty so it's even with the surrounding wood surfaces.

The keys to getting a satisfactory finish are to do careful, thorough prep work; make a wise finishing product choice; and follow the product manufacturer's directions closely when applying the product. When clear-finishing or staining a plywood project, condition the wood first (See photos, below). See page 10 for advice and tips on matching an original wood finish and for deciding whether to finish your built-in project before, after or during the assembly process.

Tips for sanding sheet goods

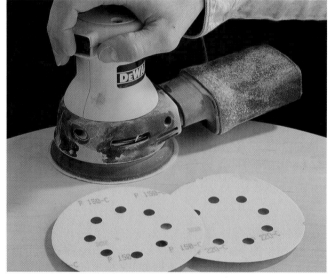

Use a random-orbit sander with dust extraction for most of your finish sanding. This type of sander leaves minimal sanding marks. With sheet goods, it's seldom necessary to sand past 150-grit.

Avoid oversanding. Face veneer on most American and Canadian produced plywood is about 1/32 in. thick. Even when using medium or fine sandpaper, it doesn't take long to sand through the face veneer.

Wood surface preparation methods compared

Liquid stain applied over untreated pine veneer looks blotchy and dark, and stain penetration is hard to control.

Liquid stain applied over pine treated with a wash coat of commercial wood conditioner (can use diluted shellac instead) has even color penetration and is lighter in tone.

Gel stain applied over untreated pine also provides even color penetration since gel stains do not penetrate wood surfaces as deeply as liquid stains.

Visual reference chart: Common wood stain tones applied to plywood

PINE PLYWOOD	OAK PLYWOOD
Clear topcoat only	Clear topcoat only
Light stain	Light stain
Medium stain	Medium stain
Dark stain	Dark stain

Corner China Cabinet (126)

Window Seat with Shelving (86)

Utility Locker (98)

Room Divider (106)

Custom Closet (118)

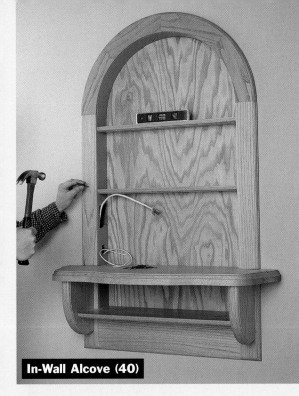
In-Wall Alcove (40)

Home Theater (140)

Laundry Center (52)

Breakfast Booth (24)

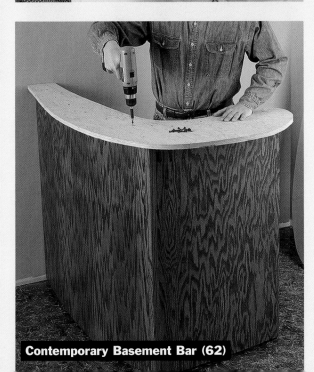
Contemporary Basement Bar (62)

Floor-to-Ceiling Bookcase (76)

Breakfast Booth

Capture the charm of your favorite diner or coffee shop in an efficient 4 × 6 footprint when you build this breakfast booth. It makes great use of limited space and provides a cozy spot for family meals. Better still, there's plenty of knee room, thanks to a metal table substructure that supports the table, eliminating the need for a table leg. The booth seats four adults comfortably, and its laminated top makes cleanup a breeze.

Vital statistics

TYPE: Breakfast booth

OVERALL SIZE: $71\frac{7}{8}$L by $36\frac{1}{2}$H by $50\frac{5}{8}$D

MATERIAL: Maple plywood and lumber, poplar beadboard, fir plywood, particleboard, plastic laminate, steel tubing, plate steel

JOINERY: Butt joints reinforced with glue and screws

CONSTRUCTION DETAILS:
- Metal table substructure bolts to the wall and is concealed behind a plywood wall backer and poplar beadboard
- Base molding and caps receive routed $\frac{1}{8}$-in.-radius beaded bit profiles
- Table consists of particleboard with built-up edging, covered with laminate
- Steel table substructure is easy to weld or inexpensive to have fabricated
- Table fastens to metal substructure with carriage bolts driven through the table stretchers

FINISH: Primer and paint; clear polyurethane

Building time

PREPARING STOCK: 1-2 hours

LAYOUT: 3-4 hours

CUTTING PARTS: 4-6 hours

ASSEMBLY: 4-6 hours

TABLETOP: 2-4 hours

FINISHING: 4-6 hours

INSTALLATION: 4-6 hours

TOTAL: 22-34 hours

Shopping List

- [ ] (3) $\frac{3}{4}$ in. × 4 × 8 ft. maple plywood
- [ ] (1) $\frac{3}{4}$ in. × 4 × 8 ft. fir plywood
- [ ] (1) $\frac{3}{4}$ in. × 4 × 4 ft. particleboard
- [ ] (6) $\frac{3}{4}$ × 6 in. × 8 ft. maple
- [ ] $\frac{3}{8}$ in. poplar beadboard; 30 sq. ft., plus waste
- [ ] (1) $\frac{1}{4}$ in. × 4 × 4 ft. untempered hardboard
- [ ] Steel table substructure (See page 28)
- [ ] (1) 32 × 50 in. plastic laminate, minimum, without edging
- [ ] Laminate edging; $1\frac{3}{4}$ in. × 11 lin. ft. (or cut from larger laminate sheet)
- [ ] Drywall screws ($1\frac{1}{4}$-, $1\frac{1}{2}$-, 2-, 3-, $3\frac{1}{2}$-in.)
- [ ] 3 in. wall anchors
- [ ] (20) $\frac{1}{4}$ × $2\frac{1}{2}$ in. lag screws, washers
- [ ] (4) $\frac{1}{4}$ × 3 in. carriage bolts, washers, nuts
- [ ] Wood glue
- [ ] Contact cement
- [ ] Finishing materials

Breakfast Booth

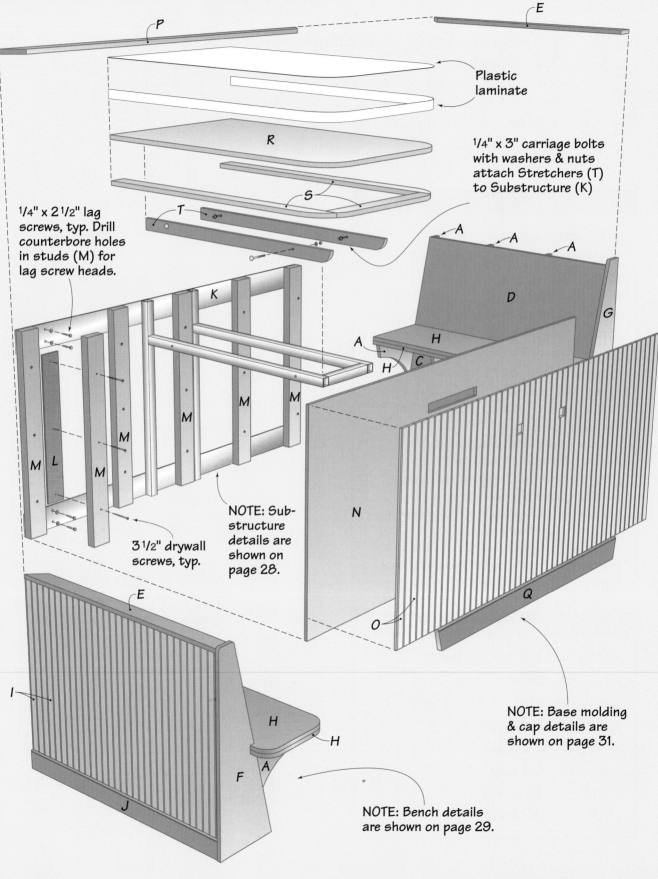

Plastic laminate

1/4" x 3" carriage bolts with washers & nuts attach Stretchers (T) to Substructure (K)

1/4" x 2 1/2" lag screws, typ. Drill counterbore holes in studs (M) for lag screw heads.

3 1/2" drywall screws, typ.

NOTE: Substructure details are shown on page 28.

NOTE: Base molding & cap details are shown on page 31.

NOTE: Bench details are shown on page 29.

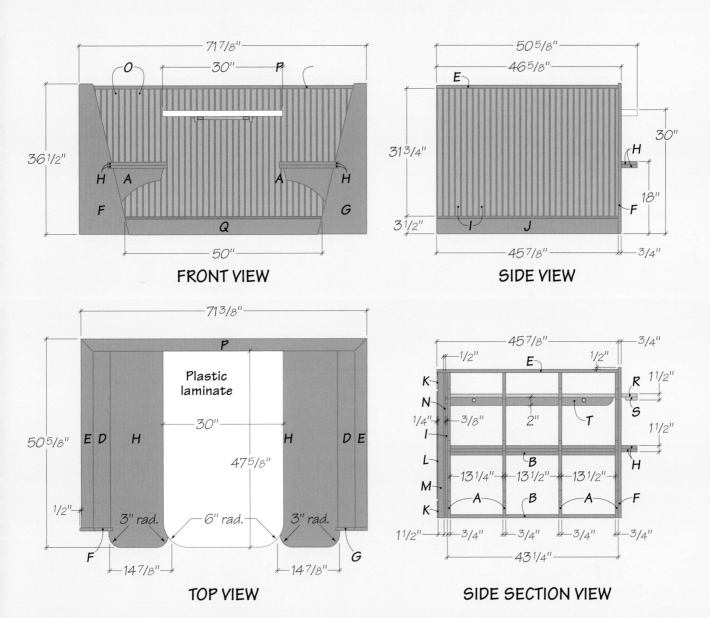

FRONT VIEW

SIDE VIEW

TOP VIEW

SIDE SECTION VIEW

Breakfast Booth Cutting List

Part	No.	Size	Material
BENCHES			
A. Supports	8	¾ × 20¼ × 35¼ in.	Maple plywood
B. Stretchers	12	¾ × 2½ × 43¼ in.	Maple
C. Kick panels	2	¾ × 16⅜ × 43¼ in.	Maple plywood
D. Seat backs	2	¾ × 18⁵⁄₁₆ × 43¼ in.	"
E. Caps	2	¾ × 3 × 45⅞ in.	Maple
F. Finished end (Room-side)	1	¾ × 12½ × 36½ in.	Maple plywood
G. Finished end (Wall-side)	1	¾ × 12⅛ × 36½ in.	"
H. Seats	4	¾ × 14⅞ × 48 in.	"
I. Finished back	1	⅜ × 45⅜ × 31¾ in.	Poplar beadboard
J. Base molding	1	¾ × 3½ × 45⅞ in.	Maple

Part	No.	Size	Material
BACK WALL			
K. Substructure	1	See drawings	Welded steel
L. Stud shims	6	¼ × 3½ × 26 in.	Hardboard
M. Studs	6	1½ × 3½ × 35¼ in.	Fir
N. Backer	1	½ × 35¼ × 71 in.	Plywood
O. Face	1	⅜ × 71 × 31¾ in.	Poplar beadboard
P. Cap	1	¾ × 3 × 71½ in.	Maple
Q. Base molding	1	¾ × 3½ × 50 in.	"
TABLE			
R. Top	1	¾ × 30 × 48 in.	Particleboard
S. Edging	3	¾ × 3 × varies	"
T. Stretchers	2	¾ × 2 × 42 in.	Maple

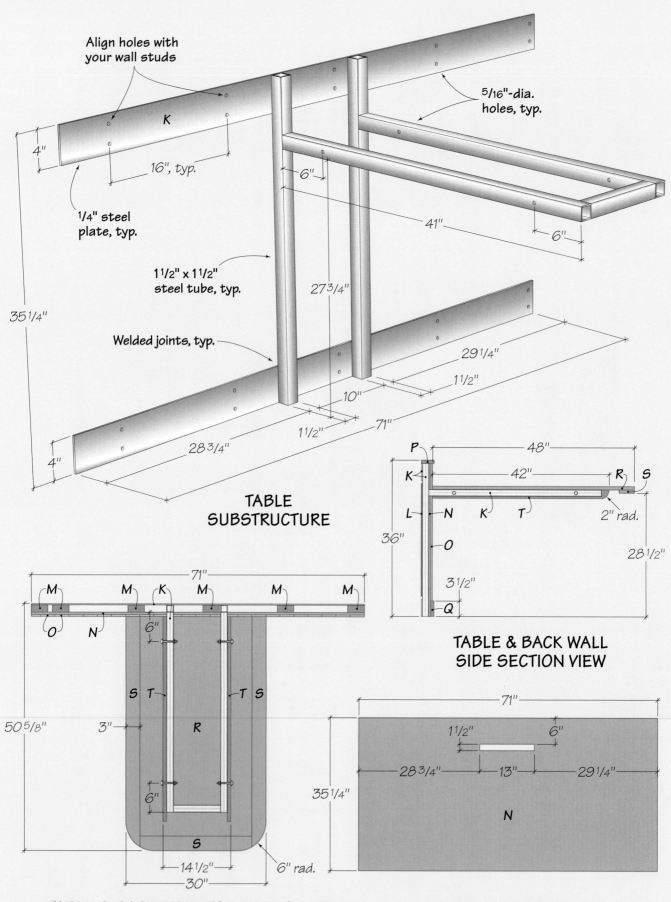

Align holes with
your wall studs

K

4"

16", typ.

5/16"-dia.
holes, typ.

1/4" steel
plate, typ.

6"

41"

6"

1 1/2" x 1 1/2"
steel tube, typ.

27 3/4"

35 1/4"

Welded joints, typ.

29 1/4"

1 1/2"

10"

28 3/4"

1 1/2"

71"

4"

TABLE
SUBSTRUCTURE

71"

M   M   K   M   M   M

6"

O   N

S T   T S

R

50 5/8"

3"

6"

S

14 1/2"

6" rad.

30"

TABLE & BACK WALL TOP SECTION VIEW

P   48"

K   42"   R S

L   N   K   T   2" rad.

36"

O   28 1/2"

3 1/2"

Q

TABLE & BACK WALL
SIDE SECTION VIEW

71"

1 1/2"   6"

28 3/4"   13"   29 1/4"

35 1/4"

N

WALL BACKER (N)

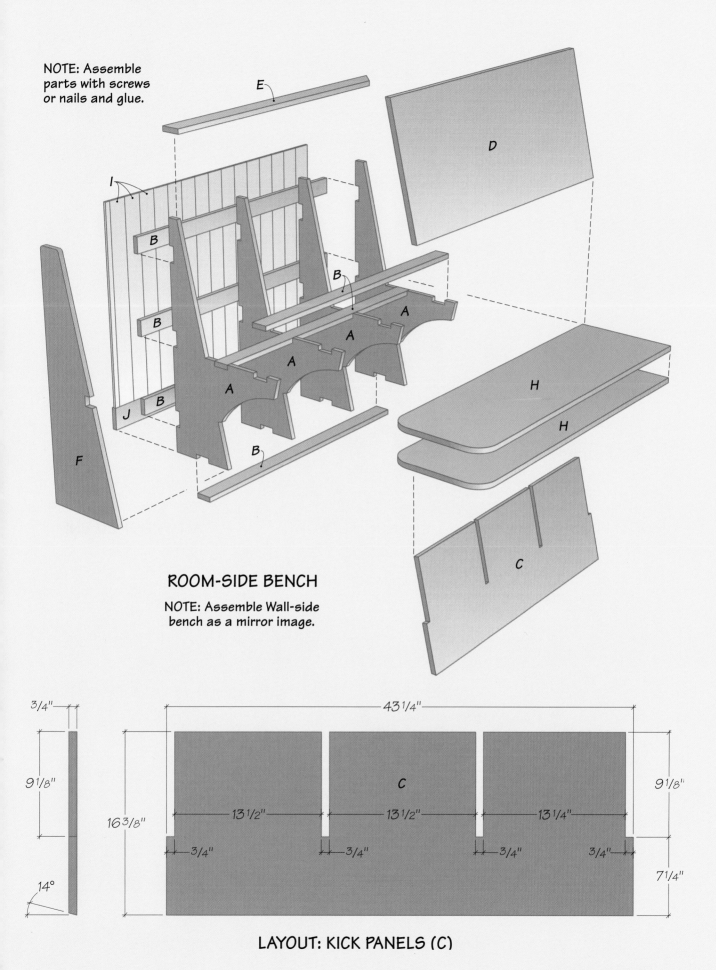

NOTE: Assemble parts with screws or nails and glue.

E

I

D

B

B

B

B

A

A

A

A

B

J

F

B

H

H

C

ROOM-SIDE BENCH

NOTE: Assemble Wall-side bench as a mirror image.

3/4"

9 1/8"

14°

43 1/4"

16 3/8"

C

13 1/2"   13 1/2"   13 1/4"

3/4"   3/4"   3/4"   3/4"

9 1/8"

7 1/4"

LAYOUT: KICK PANELS (C)

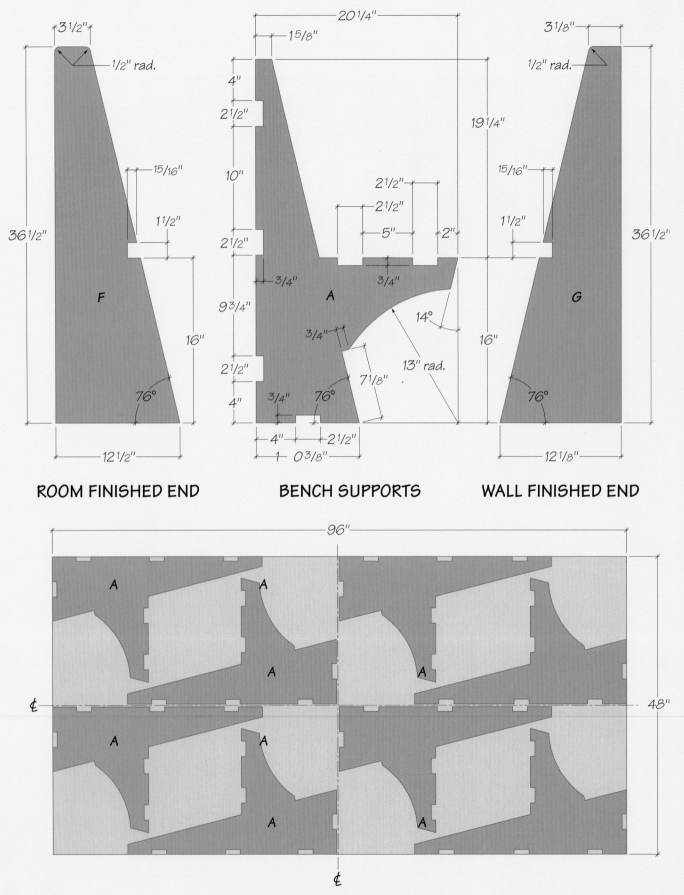

ROOM FINISHED END   BENCH SUPPORTS   WALL FINISHED END

LAYOUT: BENCH SUPPORTS (A)

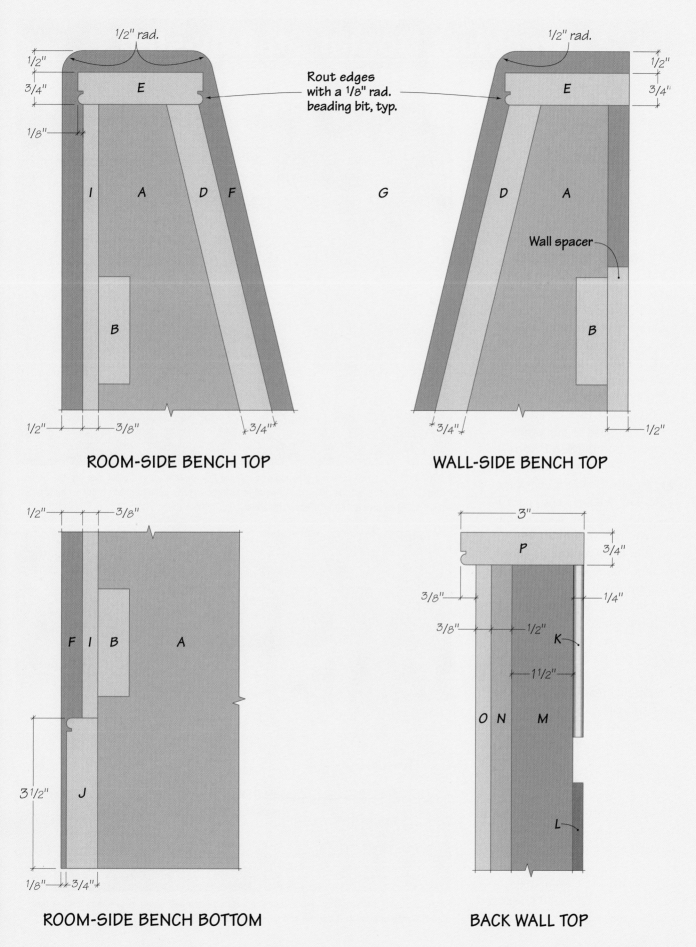

½" rad.

½"

¾"

⅛"

½" rad.

Rout edges
with a ⅛" rad.
beading bit, typ.

½"

¾"

E

I   A   D   F

B

½"   3/8"   ¾"

ROOM-SIDE BENCH TOP

E

G   D   A

Wall spacer

B

¾"   ½"

WALL-SIDE BENCH TOP

½"   3/8"

F I B   A

3½"   J

⅛"   ¾"

ROOM-SIDE BENCH BOTTOM

3"

P   ¾"

3/8"   ¼"

3/8"   ½"   K

1½"

O N   M

L

BACK WALL TOP

BUILD THE BENCHES

1 Make a template for the bench supports. Use a piece of scrap ¼-in. plywood, hardboard or the remainder of the ½-in. sheet you'll use for making the wall backer. Follow the *Bench Supports* drawing, page 30, and draw the outline. To draw the arc on the wood pattern, use a trammel, string compass or adjustable trammel points (**See Photo A**).

2 Lay out the eight bench supports. For ease in handling, cut a 4 × 8-ft. sheet of ¾-in. maple plywood in half lengthwise. Position the supports as shown in the *Layout: Bench Supports* diagram, page 30, and use the template to trace four supports on each half-sheet.

3 Cut out the bench supports with a jig saw (**See Photo B**). The angled leading ends of the seat supports and the arched lower edges will be exposed when the project is fully assembled, so fill any voids in these edges with wood putty and sand them well.

4 Cut and attach the stretchers. We used maple, but since the stretchers are not visible when the nook is finished you could use any hardwood or even strips of ¾-in. plywood. Rip and crosscut the 12 pieces of ¾ × 2½-in. stock

PHOTO A: Use a piece of scrap plywood or hardboard to make a template for drawing the bench supports. Draw the outline, using a trammel, a string compass or adjustable trammel points (as shown here) to create the arc below the seats.

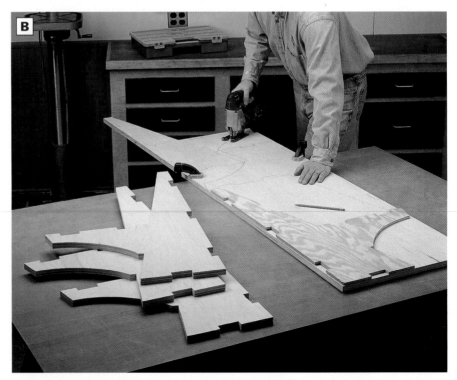

PHOTO B: Using the template, trace four supports on each half-sheet of plywood. Secure the material with clamps and cut out the supports with your jig saw.

to length. Measure and mark screw locations on the stretchers, using the *Side Section View* drawing, page 27, as a guide for spacing the holes. Attach the stretchers to the bench supports with glue and countersunk 1¾-in. drywall screws, fastening the seat stretchers first, then the bottom stretcher, then the back stretchers **(See Photo C)**. The outermost bench supports on each bench should be held flush with the ends of the stretchers. Assemble both bench frames.

5 Make the two kick panels. Rip a 17-in.-wide, 8-ft.-long blank from a sheet of ¾-in. maple plywood. Trim the blank to 16⅜ in. final width by bevel-ripping one long edge at a 14° angle. Cut the panels to length and lay out the notches (See *Layout: Kick Panels,* page 29), using a framing square to keep the four notches perpendicular to the top (square) edges. Cut out the notches with a jig saw **(See Photo D)**.

6 Install the kick panels. Lay each bench on its back and fit the kick panel into place. Fasten the parts with glue and finish nails.

7 Make the seats. Cut four identical seat blanks to size from ¾-in. maple plywood. Draw 3-in. radii on two corners of one blank, cut out the curved shapes and use this blank as a template for drawing the seat shape onto the other three blanks. Cut the remaining seat blanks to shape.

8 Assemble and attach the seats to the benches. First glue up pairs of seat blanks and reinforce the joints with 1¼-in. screws. Drill countersunk pilot holes, and drive all the screws from the same side. Fill the exposed plywood edges with putty and sand them smooth. Position the seats on the bench supports with the wall ends flush and the screwed faces down. Drill countersunk pilot holes up through the seat stretchers, and fasten the seats to the benches with 2-in. screws driven through the stretchers **(See Photo E)**.

9 Make the two finished ends. The finished end for the wall side is slightly narrower than the finished end for the room side because the wall bench has no back or wall cap overhang. Use the *Finished End* drawings, page 30, to lay out and cut the booth finished end to size and shape from maple plywood. Cut a back-bevel on the wall-side finished end along the edge that meets the wall, if you plan to scribe and trim this edge for a tight fit to the wall. Stop the bevel ¾ in. from the top of the finished end.

PHOTO C: Attach the stretchers to the bench supports with glue and screws. It's easiest if you attach the seat stretchers first, then the bottom stretcher and finish up with the back stretchers.

PHOTO D: Lay out the kick panel notches with a framing square, and cut them with a jig saw. You'll need to drill a hole near one bottom corner of each notch to provide clearance for turning the saw in the cut.

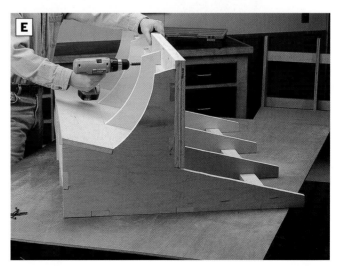

PHOTO E: Fasten the seats to the bench supports by driving screws up through the bench stretchers.

PHOTO F: Attach the finished ends with screws from inside the outer bench supports. Refer to the *Bench Top* drawings, page 31, for establishing the proper overhangs of these ends on the benches. Use clamps to hold the ends in place while you fasten them.

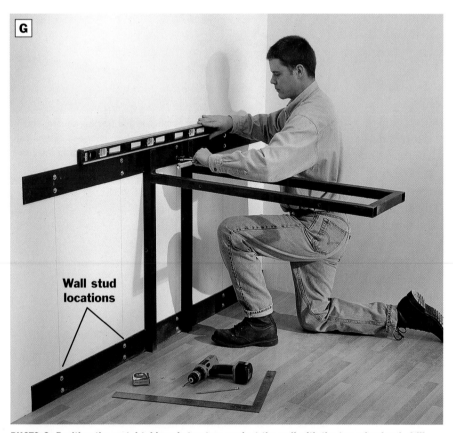

Wall stud locations

PHOTO G: Position the metal table substructure against the wall with the top edge level, drill pilot holes, and use a ratchet to drive ¼ × 2½-in. lag screws into the wall studs.

10 Attach the finished ends. Position the finished ends on the benches as follows: On the room-side bench, allow the back edge of the finished end to overhang the back edge of the outermost bench support by ⅞ in. For the wall-side bench, the finished end overhangs the bench support back edge by ½ in. Align the bottoms of the finished ends with the bench bottoms. Attach the finished ends to the benches with countersunk 1¼-in. screws driven through the bench supports (**See Photo F**).

11 Finish the bench structures. Fill screw head recesses and sand the surfaces smooth. Finish the benches with primer and paint.

BUILD THE BACK WALL

The back wall conceals a welded steel substructure that supports the table. Before making or ordering the substructure, locate the centerlines of the studs in the installation wall so you can accurately determine the locations of the lag screw holes in the steel plates. The substructure is designed to fit tight into the room corner and be flush with the end of the booth wall.

12 Make the substructure or have it built by a metal fabricator. The frame is built from ¼ × 4-in. plate steel and ³⁄₁₆ × 1½ × 1½-in. steel tubing (See the *Table Substructure* drawing, page 28). Note that the table supports are off-centered left to right on the steel plates by ½ in. to allow for the ⅜-in. beadboard and the ⅛-in. cap overhang that occur only on the room bench. NOTE: *If you choose to have someone make the substructure for you, supply them with a copy of the drawing and spacing requirements for the wall stud lag screw holes.*

13 Install the substructure. Hold it tight against the room corner, resting on the floor. Level the top edge, drill ¼-in.-dia. pilot holes into the studs and drive 2½-in. lag screws with a ratchet to fasten the substructure (**See Photo G**). File off any sharp corners.

14 Make and install the back wall studs and shims, which provide a nailing surface for the backer. First cut the stud shims to size from ¼-in. material. Next, cut the studs to length from 2 × 4 stock. The backs of the studs must be counterbored to fit over the heads of the lag screws. To do this, stand each stud in its place (See *Table & Back Wall Top Section View,* page 28) and use a hammer to tap the face of the stud at the top and bottom so the screw heads leave impressions in the stud backs. Use a ¾-in. spade bit to drill ⅜-in.-deep recesses at each screw head location. Slip shims behind the studs and fasten the parts to the wall with 3½-in. drywall screws or wall anchors (**See Photo H**).

15 Cut the backer to size from ½-in. plywood. Confirm the actual size and location of the table support slot, draw the outline and cut out the slot with your jig saw. Attach the backer to the studs with 1½-in. drywall screws.

16 Make the baseboard. Choose clear, straight ¾-in. maple, and rip enough 3½-in.-wide stock to make the back wall and room-side base molding. Rout a ⅛-in. radius bead profile into the faces of both lengths of base molding, along one long edge (See *Room-Side Bench Bottom* drawing, page 31).

17 Install the wall beadboard. Stand the baseboard along the

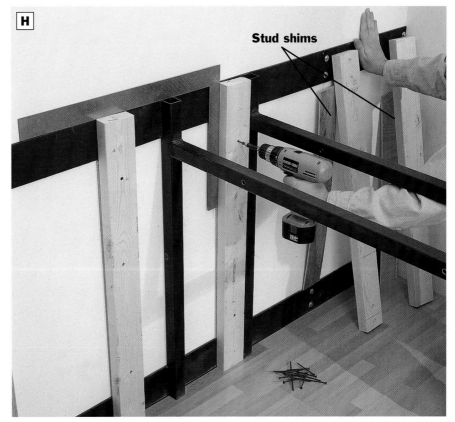

PHOTO H: Install the back wall studs over ¼-in.-thick shims using 3-in. drywall screws or wall anchors. You'll need to drill shallow counterbores in the studs so they'll fit over the screw heads.

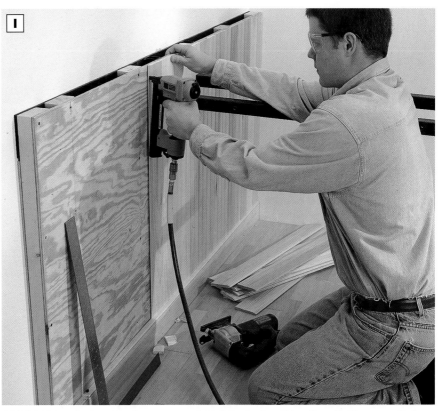

PHOTO I: Using the baseboard as a spacer, install the back wall beadboard with pneumatic fasteners or finish nails. Trim those beadboard pieces that fit around the steel table supports with a jig saw.

PHOTO J: After the room-side bench has been positioned and leveled, secure it with screws driven into the wall and floor.

K

PHOTO K: Temporarily position the baseboard as a spacer, and attach the finished back beadboard to the room-side bench with a nail gun or standard finish nails.

floor to serve as a spacer. Confirm the exact length of the beadboard sections so they'll be flush with the top of the backer and studs. Cut the beadboard pieces carefully to length and attach them to the wall backer with a nail gun or hammer and finish nails (**See Photo I**). Drive the nails at an angle along the base of the tongues—not the grooves. The angle will keep the tongues from splitting. Use a jig saw to trim those beadboard pieces that wrap around the metal table support tubes. Remove the baseboard.

⑱ Finish the beadboard wall with primer and paint.

INSTALL THE BENCHES

⑲ Install the wall-side bench. This bench is attached both to the room wall and the back booth wall. Set the bench in place and level it with shims. If the room wall is straight, make wall spacers from ½-in. plywood scrap and insert them behind the bench stretchers before fastening the bench to the wall. If the wall is not straight, use tapered shims as needed to provide a solid attachment surface. Scribe and trim the finished end, so the bench fits tightly against the wall (See page 15). Install the bench with 3-in. screws driven into both walls.

⑳ Install the room-side bench. Slide the bench into place so the back of the bench structure is flush with the end of the back wall. Check to make sure the bench is level and even with the top edge of the back wall. Adjust with shims, if necessary. Install the bench with 3-in. screws driven into the back wall and floor (**See Photo J**).

㉑ Cut and fit the wall baseboard.

Set it aside to be finished with the cap pieces before installation.

㉒ Install the finished back beadboard. Start by cutting the bench baseboard to length and temporarily positioning it along the floor as a spacer. Confirm the length of the beadboard sections, cut them to length and attach with a nail gun or finish nails **(See Photo K)**. Scribe and rip the last piece to width for a tight fit. Remove the baseboard. Finish the beadboard bench back with primer and paint.

㉓ Make and attach the seat backs. Cut the two plywood backs to size, with the top and bottom edges beveled at 14°. NOTE: *This is most accurately done by starting with blanks that are slightly wide, beveling the bottom edges, fitting the blanks on the benches, then beveling the top edges. It is important that the top edges of the seat backs be flush with the tops of the bench supports in order to form a tight joint beneath the caps.* After fitting and sizing the parts, remove them and apply primer and paint. Then attach the seat backs to the benches with finish nails, and conceal the nailheads with putty and paint.

㉔ Make the wall and bench caps. Cut these three pieces slightly long and rout the ⅛-in.-radius beaded profiles **(See Photo L)**. Note that the cap for the room-side bench is beaded along both bottom edges while the caps that butt against the two walls are profiled only along the inside bottom edge (See *Room-Side Bench Top* and *Wall-Side Bench Top* drawings, page 31). After routing the beaded edges, cut the cap pieces to length and miter-cut the corner joints.

PHOTO L: Mill the edges of the bench and wall caps on the router table with a ⅛-in. piloted beading bit. For safety's sake, always use featherboards and push pads or sticks when machining small or narrow pieces.

PHOTO M: Install the prefinished cap pieces with a nail gun or standard finish nails, taking care to keep the mitered corner joints tight and flush.

PHOTO N: Fasten the edging strips to the underside of the tabletop with glue and screws. Locate the screws so they will not interfere with cutting the 6-in. radii on the table corners.

PHOTO O: Clamp the top stretchers in place against the metal table supports and mark the carriage bolt hole locations with a pencil. Drill the bolt holes using a 5⁄16-in. bit and a drill guide to ensure that the holes are straight.

PHOTO P: With the stretchers clamped to the table supports, center the table between the benches, mark the stretcher centerlines, and drill countersunk pilot holes. Lift up the tabletop, apply glue to the stretchers, then fasten the top to the stretchers with 1½-in. drywall screws.

㉕ Topcoat the caps and base molding with a protective finish—we used polyurethane. Fasten the caps and base molding with a nail gun or finish nails **(See Photo M)**. Recess the nailheads with a nailset and fill the voids with putty stick.

BUILD & INSTALL THE TABLE

The table consists of a piece of particleboard built up around the lower edges with particleboard strips to give it a more substantial look and to hide the metal supports beneath. Plastic laminate covers the edges and tabletop to provide a sanitary surface that's easy to keep clean. Maple stretchers beneath the tabletop create a fastening surface for bolts and nuts that attach it to the metal substructure. You'll build the table to completion before installing it.

㉖ Make the table. Cut the tabletop to size from ¾-in. particleboard. Cut the edging strips and attach them to the table blank with glue and screws **(See Photo N)**, taking care that the joints are tight and that no screws interfere with cutting the radii on the corners. Mark 6-in. arcs on the outside corners and cut the table to shape with a jig saw. Sand the curved edges.

㉗ Rip and crosscut the table stretchers to size, then cut a 2-in.-radius arc into each bottom outside corner. Sand the edges well. Clamp the stretchers in place against the table support and mark the bolt hole locations with an awl or pencil. Drill the bolt holes using a 5⁄16-in. bit and a drill guide to ensure that the holes are straight **(See Photo O)**.

㉘ Attach the table to the stretchers. Re-clamp the stretchers in place against the table supports. Position the table on the stretchers, centering it between the benches. Measure and mark the stretcher centerlines on the tabletop. Lift up the top, apply glue to the stretchers, reposition the top and fasten it to the stretchers with countersunk 1½-in. drywall screws (**See Photo P**).

㉙ Laminate the table. Apply the plastic laminate edging first, spreading contact cement evenly along the table edge and the back of the laminate. If a joint is necessary, keep it away from the radiused corners. Trim the top and bottom edges of the edging flush with a router and piloted laminate-trimming bit. Apply the laminate to the top, first sizing the laminate sheet so it overhangs the top by ½ to 1 in. in each direction. Spread contact cement over the tabletop surface, and when the contact cement is dry lay spacer strips on the table to help you position the laminate carefully. Coat the back of the laminate with contact cement, let it dry and set it into place. Remove the strips one at a time, pressing down the laminate with your hand. After all the strips have been removed, roll the laminate with a J-roller to remove any air bubbles and ensure a good bond with the adhesive, then trim the laminate flush (**See Photo Q**).

㉚ Install the table. Position the table over the metal supports, insert carriage bolts through the stretcher holes, and fasten the table with washers and nuts (**See Photo R**). The inset photo clearly shows the installation scheme, with the rounded heads of the carriage bolts facing the outside of the table stretchers.

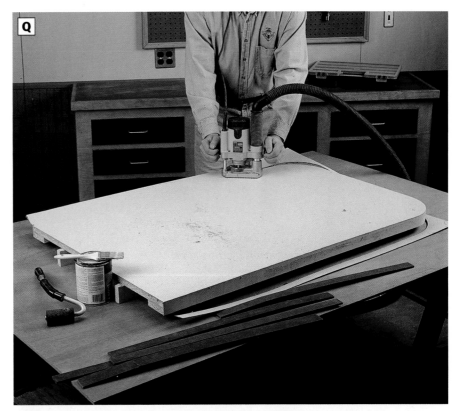

PHOTO Q: After applying the laminate to the tabletop and rolling it thoroughly with a J-roller, trim off the excess laminate with a router and piloted laminate-trimming bit.

PHOTO R: Install the table with carriage bolts, nuts and washers. Tighten the fasteners with a ratchet. INSET PHOTO: Note how the rounded heads of the carriage bolts are on the outside of the table stretchers with the nuts inside the metal supports. This way, knees and clothing are protected from metal corners and edges.

In-Wall Alcove

Remember those charming older homes with a telephone niche built into the wall? With this as our inspiration, we designed an alcove that can be retrofitted into just about any home and combines all the essentials of a contemporary message center. Our alcove has ample counter space for a phone, answering machine, note pad and maybe even a small lamp. In addition, it has a handy lower shelf for phone books and two display shelves for family photos or treasured mementos. If a phone center isn't what you need, build the alcove for use as a home mail organizer or even an entry room valet.

Vital statistics

TYPE: Wall-cavity alcove

OVERALL SIZE: 35W by 50¾H by 15½D

MATERIAL: Red oak lumber and plywood, untempered hardboard

JOINERY: Butt joints reinforced with dowels, glue and screws

CONSTRUCTION DETAILS:
· Face frame segments joined with dowels
· Curved face frame cut with a router and circle-cutting jig
· Outer edges of face frame and counter receive beaded and classic ogee routed profiles
· Interior curved wall made of untempered hardboard bent into shape
· Project designed to fit into a 2 × 4-framed stud wall, with studs spaced 16 in. on-center. One intermediate wall stud will need to be removed to install the project

FINISH: Stain, polyurethane varnish, paint

Building time

PREPARING STOCK: 2-3 hours

LAYOUT: 2-4 hours

CUTTING PARTS: 4-6 hours

ASSEMBLY: 3-5 hours

FINISHING: 2-4 hours

INSTALLATION: 2-4 hours

TOTAL: 15-26 hours

Shopping List

- [ ] (1) ¾ in. × 2 × 4 ft. red oak plywood
- [ ] (1) 8/4 × 8 in. × 8 ft. red oak
- [ ] (1) ¾ × 6 in. × 8 ft. red oak
- [ ] (2) ¾ × 4 in. × 8 ft. red oak
- [ ] (1) ¼ × 4⅛ in. × 8 ft. untempered hardboard
- [ ] (22) dowels, ⅜-in.-dia. × 1½ in.
- [ ] Drywall screws (1-, 1¼-, 1⅝-in.)
- [ ] Wood glue
- [ ] Telephone jack, cover, phone wire
- [ ] Electrical box, outlet, cover, wire
- [ ] Finishing materials

In-Wall Alcove

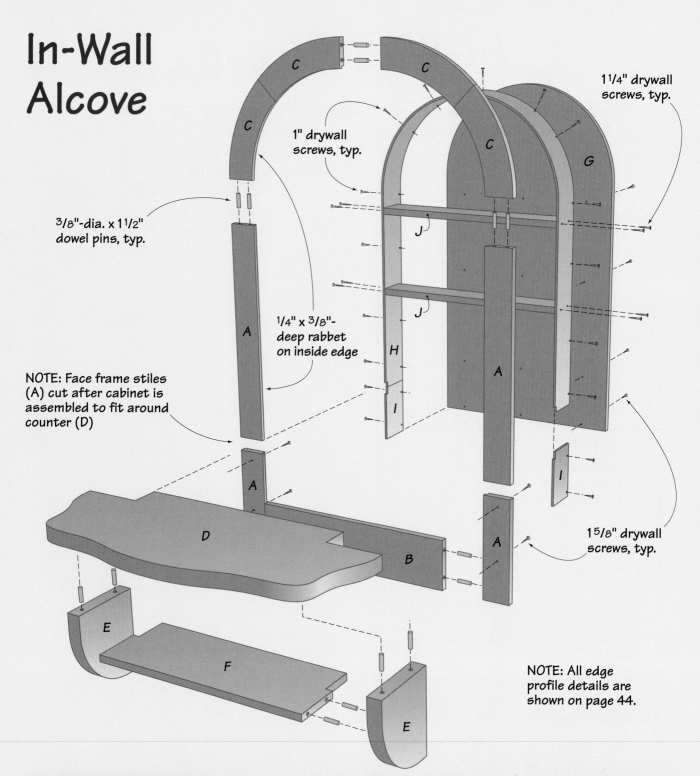

1 1/4" drywall screws, typ.

1" drywall screws, typ.

3/8"-dia. x 1 1/2" dowel pins, typ.

1/4" x 3/8"-deep rabbet on inside edge

NOTE: Face frame stiles (A) cut after cabinet is assembled to fit around counter (D)

1 5/8" drywall screws, typ.

NOTE: All edge profile details are shown on page 44.

In-Wall Alcove Cutting List

Part	No.	Size	Material
A. Stiles	2	3/4 × 3 × 36 1/4 in.	Red oak
B. Bottom rail	1	3/4 × 5 1/2 × 23 in.	"
C. Arc segments	4	3/4 × 4 1/2 × 12 in.	"
D. Counter	1	1 1/2 × 14 3/4 × 35 in.	"
E. Braces	2	1 1/2 × 7 3/4 × 8 3/4 in.	"
F. Lower shelf	1	3/4 × 9 × 24 1/2 in.	"
G. Back	1	3/4 × 23 × 42 1/4 in.	Oak plywood
H. Upper interior wall	1	1/4 × 4 1/8 × 84 3/4 in.	Hardboard
I. Lower interior walls	2	1/4 × 4 1/8 × 6 1/2 in.	"
J. Upper shelves	2	3/4 × 3 3/8 × 23 in.	Red oak

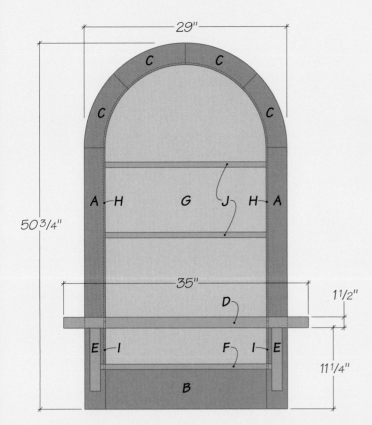

FRONT VIEW

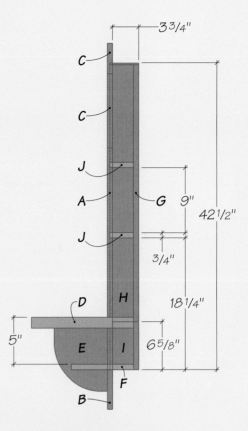

SIDE SECTION VIEW

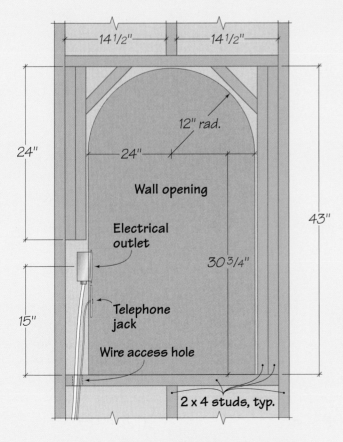

WALL OPENING FRAMING

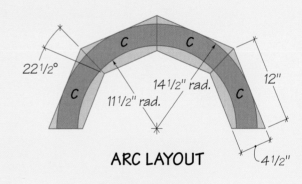

ARC LAYOUT

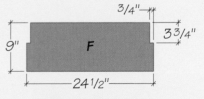

LOWER SHELF

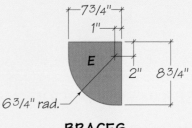

BRACES

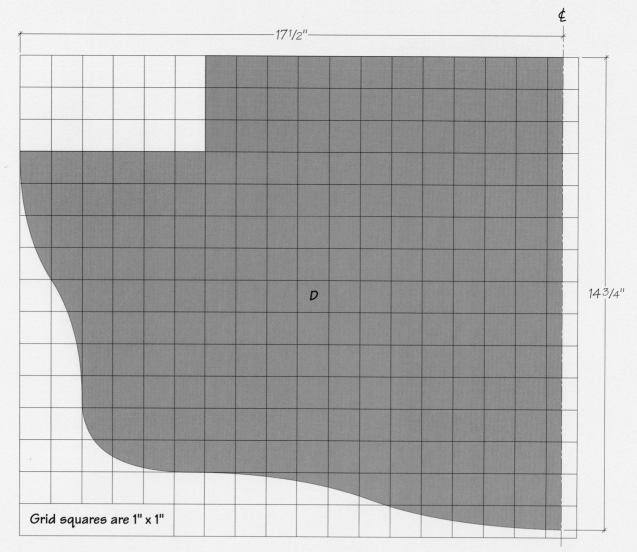

17 1/2"

¢

14 3/4"

D

Grid squares are 1" x 1"

COUNTER LAYOUT

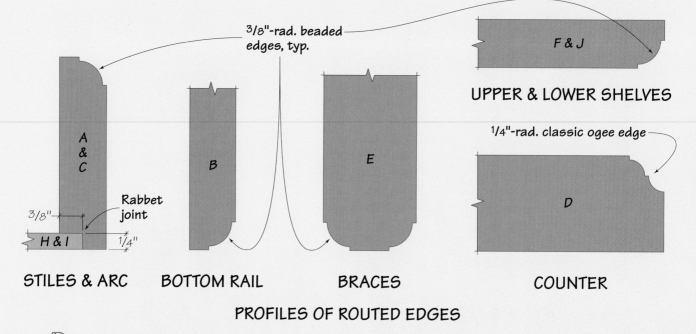

3/8"-rad. beaded
edges, typ.

F & J

UPPER & LOWER SHELVES

A
&
C

B

E

1/4"-rad. classic ogee edge

D

Rabbet
joint

3/8"

H & I

1/4"

STILES & ARC   BOTTOM RAIL   BRACES   COUNTER

PROFILES OF ROUTED EDGES

MAKE THE FACE FRAME

❶ Rip and crosscut the stiles and bottom rail to size. Rip and crosscut the four arc segments to size, then miter-cut both ends of each segment at a 22½° angle. The long edge of each arc segment should be 12 in. long.

❷ Drill pairs of dowel holes for the face frame joints. Lay the face frame pieces in position on your worksurface, and use a pencil to mark two dowel hole locations across each joint. Use a doweling jig as a guide, and drill a ⅜-in.-dia., ⅞-in.-deep dowel hole at each dowel mark **(See Photo A)**.

❸ Assemble the frame. Apply glue to the dowels and tap them into their holes with a wood mallet. Spread glue on the mating surfaces and join all the face frame pieces together. Clamp the frame together with a strap clamp until the glue dries.

❹ Scrape away any glue squeeze-out from the face frame joints with a paint scraper, and sand the joints flush if necessary. Sanding will create a smooth surface for the router to pass over when you cut the face frame arcs.

❺ Cut the inside and outside edges of the face frame arc with a router. To do this, lay the frame on

PHOTO A: Clamp the face frame parts and use a doweling jig as a guide to drill pairs of holes for dowel joints. When marking the holes in the arc segments, keep them toward the center of the board ends so the dowels won't be trimmed away when you cut the arc later.

PHOTO B: We used a router and circle-cutting jig to cut the face frame curved profiles. Clamp the face frame to a scrap plywood panel and attach a ¾-in.-thick spacer to the center of this assembly. Attach the pivot of the circle-cutting jig to the plywood spacer at the centerpoint of the face frame arc. Use a single-fluted straight bit in the router to trim the outer face frame arc flush with the outside edges of the stiles. Reset the router jig and cut the inner arc flush with the inside edges of the stiles.

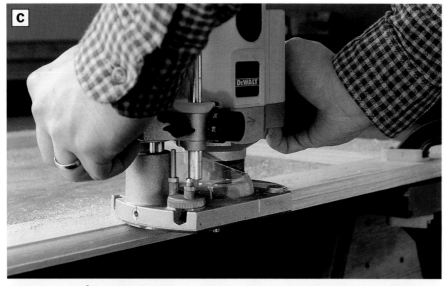

PHOTO C: Rout a ⅜-in. beaded roundover profile around the outside edge of the face frame.

PHOTO D: Use a piloted rabbeting bit to cut a ¼-in.-wide, ⅜-in.-deep rabbet around the inside back edge of the frame. The rabbet will house the interior wall of the cabinet. To provide clearance for the bit bearing, you'll need to raise the frame off the worksurface on spacer blocks.

PHOTO E: Mark the shape of the back by tracing the inside edge of the completed face frame on a piece of ¾-in. plywood. Lay the frame facedown so the rabbet will not interfere with accurate marking. Then cut the back to shape with a jig saw.

a piece of ¾-in. plywood, and secure the face frame to the plywood with clamps on the stiles and bottom rail. Determine the centerpoint of the face frame arcs on the plywood (See the *Arc Layout* drawing, page 43, for details) and position a spacer of ¾-in.-thick plywood over this centerpoint. Screw the spacer to the plywood base and mark the centerpoint on the spacer. The purpose of the spacer is to raise the circle-cutting jig pivot point to the same plane as the face frame surface. Install a straight bit in your router, attach the router to a circle-cutting jig and fix the pivot point of the router jig on the centerpoint of the spacer. Set the jig so the router will cut an arc flush with the outside edges of the stiles **(See Photo B)**. Reset the compass and cut the inner arc flush with the inside edges of the stiles. Make these cuts in passes of increasing depth (about ¼ in.) until the waste falls free.

6 Shape the entire outer edge of the face frame, using a router and piloted ⅜-in. beaded roundover bit **(See Photo C)**.

7 Rout the rabbet for the interior wall around the inside edge of the back of the frame. Clamp the frame facedown to your worksurface, and use a piloted rabbeting bit to cut this ¼-in.-wide, ⅜-in.-deep rabbet **(See Photo D)**.

BUILD THE CABINET
8 Cut the back to size, using the completed face frame as a template. Lay the frame facedown on a plywood blank, and trace around the inside edge of the frame **(See Photo E)**. Cut along the layout line with your jig saw.

9 Apply finish to the frame and back. Since the hardboard interior wall is painted with an accent color, and the wood surfaces are finished with stain and polyurethane, it is easiest to achieve clean joints if the pieces are prefinished before assembly. Sand the frame and back to 220-grit, and finish with stain and polyurethane varnish.

10 Cut the upper and lower interior wall pieces to size from ¼-in. untempered hardboard. The joints between the upper and lower wall pieces will be hidden when the counter is installed.

11 Finish the inside faces of the interior wall pieces with primer and paint.

12 Attach the interior wall to the edge of the back. Start by fastening a lower interior wall piece flush to the bottom corner of the back (painted side facing inward) with glue and countersunk 1-in. drywall screws. Then fasten the upper wall piece to the back with glue and screws, working carefully in one direction around the curve, driving screws every 6 in. and holding the hardboard in place with clamps **(See Photo F)**. Attach the other lower wall piece.

13 Attach the face frame. Spread a thin layer of glue in the rabbet and position the face frame over the interior wall. Use clamps to seat the interior wall in the rabbet, and fasten the wall in place with finish nails **(See Photo G)**.

14 Make the upper shelves. Cut a 3⅜-in.-wide oak blank for the upper shelves, about 48 in. long. Using your router and a ⅜-in. piloted bit, mill the beaded shape along one edge. Crosscut the

PHOTO F: Attach the lower and upper interior wall pieces to the edge of the back panel with glue and screws. Take extra care when bending the hardboard around the curve—it will break if bent too severely. Glue and fasten this area about 6 in. at a time, clamping the parts where you can and readjusting the clamps as you go.

PHOTO G: Set the interior wall into the face frame rabbet and fasten with glue and pin nails. Use clamps to seat the edge of the interior wall in the rabbet, and drive fasteners every 3 in. or so. You could also use a hammer, short brads and a nailset if you don't have a nail gun.

PHOTO H: Mark centerlines for screws, position the upper shelves in the cabinet with shaped edges down, drill countersunk pilot holes and fasten the shelves with 1-in. drywall screws.

PHOTO I: Trace the shape of the counter onto a 1½-in.-thick oak blank. We made a full-size hardboard template to draw the shape. Then cut out the counter.

PHOTO J: Lay out the braces on thick oak stock, cut them out with a jig saw and rout a beaded roundover profile along both curved edges of each brace. The flat edges receive no profiling.

shelves to length. Finish them to match the other wood parts.

15 Install the upper shelves. Measure and mark centerlines for screws on the outer surface of the interior walls (See the *Side Section View* drawing, page 43, for shelf locations). Arrange the shelves with the shaped edges down. Drill countersunk pilot holes and attach the shelves with 1-in. screws **(See Photo H)**.

BUILD THE COUNTER & LOWER SHELF ASSEMBLY

We made the counter and braces from ¾ oak stock, surface-planed to 1½ in. thick. You could make the counter from face-glued ¾-in. oak if thicker oak stock isn't available, but be aware that you will see a joint line on the front edges of the counter and braces.

16 Make the counter. Transfer a full-size counter pattern (See the *Counter Layout* drawing, page 44) to a scrap piece of hardboard and cut it out with a jig saw. Trace the pattern onto your oak counter blank, and cut the counter to shape **(See Photo I)**. Rout a ¼-in.-radius classic ogee around one curved edge of the counter.

17 Make the braces. Use the *Braces* drawing on page 43 to lay out two braces on 1½-in. oak stock, and cut the workpieces to size and shape with a jig saw. Using your router and piloted bit, cut the beaded roundover along both curved edges **(See Photo J)**.

18 Make the lower shelf. Edge-glue oak stock as necessary to achieve a 9-in.-wide blank, and cut the shelf to size and shape (See *Lower Shelf* drawing, page 43). Rout the beaded profile along one long shelf edge.

⑲ Measure and mark the positions for attaching the lower shelf to the braces and the braces to the counter. Locate and drill matching holes in each joint for ⅜-in.-dia., 1½-in.-long dowel pins. First drill the holes in the ends of the shelf, then use dowel points inserted into the holes to locate the corresponding holes in the sides of the braces. Next, drill the dowel holes in the top edges of the braces, insert dowel points and locate and drill corresponding holes in the underside of the counter (See Photo K).

⑳ Assemble the counter and lower shelf. Apply glue to the dowels and tap them into place. Spread glue on the ends of the shelf and clamp it into place between the braces. Spread glue on the top edges of the braces and clamp them into place against the underside of the counter (See Photo L).

㉑ Apply finish to the counter and shelf assembly. The finish should match the face frame and upper shelves.

㉒ Use the *Front View* drawing on page 43 to measure and mark the location of the counter on the face frame. Cut 1½-in. sections out of the face frame for recessing the counter into the cabinet. Make these cuts with a fine-toothed back saw to minimize tearout. You'll also need to trim ⅜-in.-deep notches out of the interior walls in the counter area (where you cut through the face frame) so the counter's back edge will fit flush against the cabinet back.

㉓ Attach the counter assembly. Slip the counter into position on the cabinet and fasten it with countersunk 1⅝-in. screws driven through the back of the face frame into the braces. Drive 1¼-in.

PHOTO K: Use dowel points to mark the holes you'll need to drill for dowel pins that attach the braces, counter and lower shelf together. A doweling jig will help you drill straight holes.

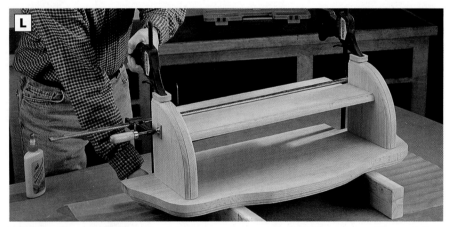

PHOTO L: After test-fitting the parts to ensure accuracy, assemble the counter and lower shelf. Spread glue on the dowels and mating joint surfaces of the lower shelf and braces, and glue and clamp these parts. Then glue up the dowel joints to secure the brace assembly to the underside of the counter.

PHOTO M: Use a fine-toothed saw to cut away 1½-in. sections of the face frame so the counter slips into the face frame and lies flush against the inside face of the cabinet back. Attach the counter assembly by drilling countersunk pilot holes and driving screws through the back of the face frame into the braces and through the interior wall into the edge of the counter.

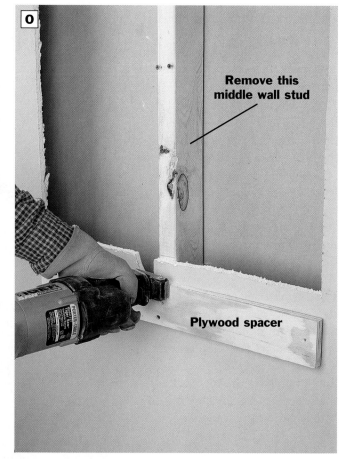

Remove this middle wall stud

Plywood spacer

PHOTO N: Set the cabinet against the wall where you plan to install it, trace around the cabinet back onto the wall, and remove this wallboard by scoring along your layout line with a utility knife. Then cut through the wallboard with a wallboard saw.

PHOTO O: Scab a piece of plywood to the wall to limit the saw's depth of cut, and cut off the middle stud 1½ in. beyond the opening at both the top and bottom (46 in. overall) to allow for the new header and sill. Avoid damaging the wallboard behind the installation area.

screws through the interior walls and into the counter as well **(See Photo M)**.

24 Cut openings for an electrical outlet (if you'll need one to power your answering machine or cordless phone charger) and phone jack into the alcove's interior wall with a jig saw or a hole saw. Install a receptacle box for the outlet.

PREPARE THE WALL FRAMING & INSTALL THE ALCOVE

We installed our alcove in a wall with studs spaced 16 in. on-center and sheathed with wallboard. Your installation and framing procedure may need to vary from the one shown here if your wall is covered with lathe and plaster or if the wall stud spacing differs.

25 Remove the wallboard from the installation area. Draw the outline of the cutout slightly larger than the back shape of the alcove. Score the outer layer of wallboard paper with a utility knife first so the wallboard doesn't tear beyond your outline when you

remove it. Then complete the cut with a wallboard saw, and remove the waste **(See Photo N)**.

26 Cut off the middle stud. First, notch the wallboard 1½ in. beyond the opening at both the top and bottom, to allow for the installation of a header and a sill. To cut the stud, we used a reciprocating saw held against a plywood spacer to keep the blade tip from puncturing the wallboard on the other side of the wall. Check your setup and blade travel before you make these cuts, then carefully cut through the stud **(See Photo O)**.

27 Remove the stud. The amount of care you need to take with this process depends on what is on the other side of the wall. If the other side is a closet or unfinished space you can just free the cut ends of the stud with a chisel and remove it, pulling nails or screws through the wallboard on the other side. If the other side is finished and visible, you may want to cut the screws or nails, using a hacksaw blade or a flexible blade in your reciprocating saw. Slip the

PHOTO P: Install the corner blocks. Measure the corners, cut pieces of 2 × 4 to size with the ends mitered at 45°, and attach the blocking pieces with drywall screws. Have an electrician extend power and a phone line to the opening.

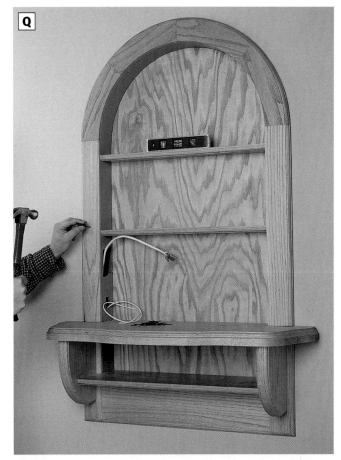

PHOTO Q: After leveling the alcove in place, install it by driving finish nails through pilot holes in the face frame and into the 2 × 4 backing pieces. Cover the nailheads with tinted wood putty.

blade between the stud and the wallboard, and saw through the screws or nails.

㉘ Complete the wall framing (See *Wall Opening Framing*, page 43). First, install the header and sill. Cut them to length, position them against the ends of the middle stud, and fasten with screws. Measure out from the side wall studs and install intermediate 2 × 4's to act as nailing surfaces for the alcove. Miter-cut two lengths of 2 × 4 blocking and screw them into the upper corners **(See Photo P)**.

㉙ Install the cabinet. Test-fit the alcove in the opening and check it for level. Shim behind it if necessary for a snug, level fit. Pull the electrical and telephone wires through their openings. Drill pilot holes through the face frame and install the alcove by driving finish nails into the stud framing **(See Photo Q)**. Set the nails and fill the holes with putty.

㉚ Connect and install the electrical outlet and the phone jack **(See Photo R)**.

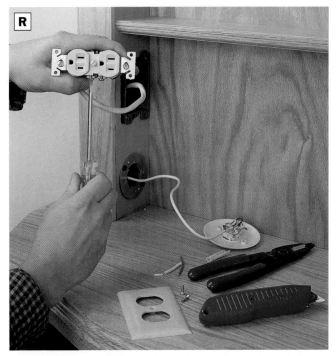

PHOTO R: Complete the installation of the electrical outlet and phone jack, then attach the covers.

Laundry Center

The area around your washer and dryer can easily become a jumble of cleaning supplies, dirty clothes, off-season storage and stranded socks. Whip that space into shape by building this clever laundry center, which provides places for laundry baskets, a counter for folding clothes, a rod for hanging shirts direct from the washing machine and lots of storage shelves—both open and enclosed. In fact, the upper cabinet is a stock item you can buy from any home center, making project construction even easier. The combination of white melamine and finished oak is as attractive as it is easy to clean, and your newly organized laundry area will make one of life's weekly chores much more pleasant.

Vital statistics

TYPE: Laundry center

OVERALL SIZE: 97L by 85⅛H by 28¼D

MATERIAL: White melamine, red oak lumber and plywood, post-formed laminate countertop, pre-fabricated upper cabinet

JOINERY: Butt joints reinforced with glue and screws, dadoes, biscuits

CONSTRUCTION DETAILS:
· Exposed edges of melamine concealed and reinforced with oak nosing
· Pre-fabricated upper cabinet simplifies construction
· Base cabinet designed to hold two standard laundry baskets
· Melamine framework erected in place on wall

FINISH: Clear polyurethane on oak parts

Building time

PREPARING STOCK: 1-2 hours

LAYOUT: 2-3 hours

CUTTING PARTS: 2-4 hours

ASSEMBLY: 4-6 hours

FINISHING: 2-3 hours

INSTALLATION: 2-4 hours

TOTAL: 13-22 hours

Shopping List

- [ ] (2) ¾ × 49 × 97 in. white melamine
- [ ] (1) ¾ in. × 4 × 8 ft. red oak plywood
- [ ] (1) ¾ × 8 in. × 10 ft. red oak
- [ ] (1) ¾ × 3½ in. × 8 ft. pine
- [ ] (1) ¼ in. × 4 × 4 ft. hardboard
- [ ] (1) 12 × 30 × 30 in. unfinished upper cabinet with doors
- [ ] (1) 1½ in. × 25 × 35¼ in. post-formed laminate countertop
- [ ] 1½-in.-dia. closet rod (3 ft.)
- [ ] Closet rod mounting sockets
- [ ] Drywall screws (2-, 1½-, 1¼-in.)
- [ ] Finish nails, #20 biscuits
- [ ] White plastic screw head covers
- [ ] Wood glue
- [ ] ¾-in. iron-on oak edge tape (15 lineal ft.)
- [ ] Finishing materials
- [ ] 24-in. under-cabinet light (optional)

Laundry Center

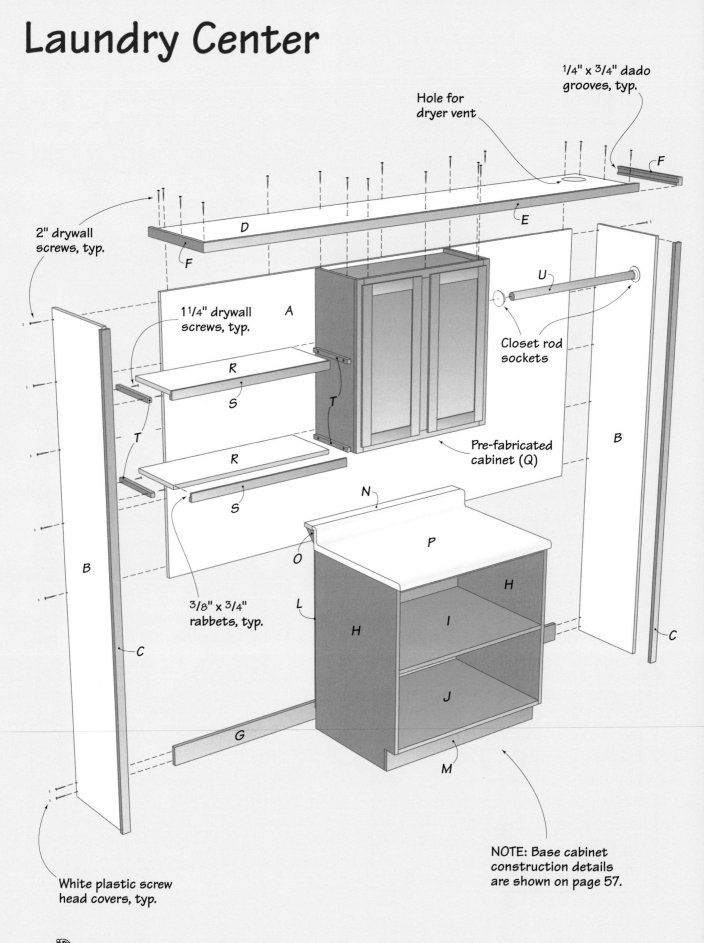

1/4" x 3/4" dado grooves, typ.

Hole for dryer vent

2" drywall screws, typ.

D

E

F

F

A

U

Closet rod sockets

1¼" drywall screws, typ.

R

S

T

B

R

T

S

Pre-fabricated cabinet (Q)

N

O

P

H

B

L

H

I

H

C

3/8" x 3/4" rabbets, typ.

J

C

G

M

White plastic screw head covers, typ.

NOTE: Base cabinet construction details are shown on page 57.

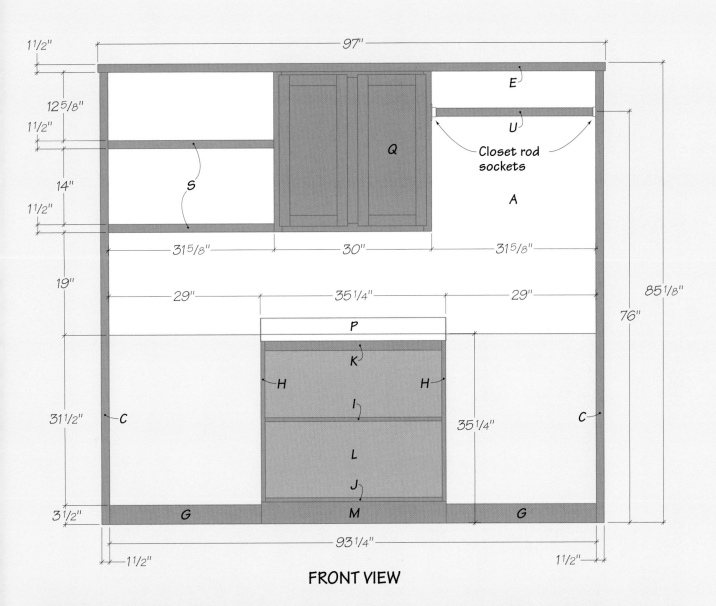

FRONT VIEW

Part	No.	Size	Material
A. Back	1	¾ × 49 × 94 in.	Melamine
B. Ends	2	¾ × 15¾ × 84 in.	"
C. End nosing	2	¾ × 1½ × 83⅝ in.	Oak
D. Top shelf	1	¾ × 16 × 96 in.	Melamine
E. Top shelf front nosing	1	¾ × 1½ × 97 in.	Oak
F. Top shelf end nosing	2	¾ × 1½ × 16½ in.	"
G. Lower stretcher	1	¾ × 3½ × 94 in.	Pine
H. Cabinet sides	2	¾ × 23¾ × 34½ in.	Oak plywood
I. Cabinet shelf	1	¾ × 23¾ × 34¼ in.	"
J. Cabinet bottom	1	¾ × 23¾ × 33¾ in.	"
K. Stretchers, hang strip	3	¾ × 2½ × 33¾ in.	"
L. Cabinet back	1	¼ × 30½ × 35¼ in.	Hardboard
M. Toe board	1	¾ × 4 × 35¼ in.	Oak plywood
N. Ledge	1	¾ × 2½ × 35¼ in.	Melamine
O. Ledge braces	4	¾ × 2½ × 2½ in.	Oak plywood
P. Countertop	1	1½ × 25 × 35¼ in.	Post-formed laminate
Q. Upper cabinet	1	12 × 30 × 30 in.	Pre-fab
R. Shelves	2	¾ × 11 × 32 in.	Melamine
S. Nosing	2	¾ × 1½ × 32 in.	Oak
T. Shelf cleats	4	¾ × ¾ × 10 in.	"
U. Closet rod	1	1½ dia. × 31¾ in.	Hardwood

Table title: **Laundry Center Cutting List**

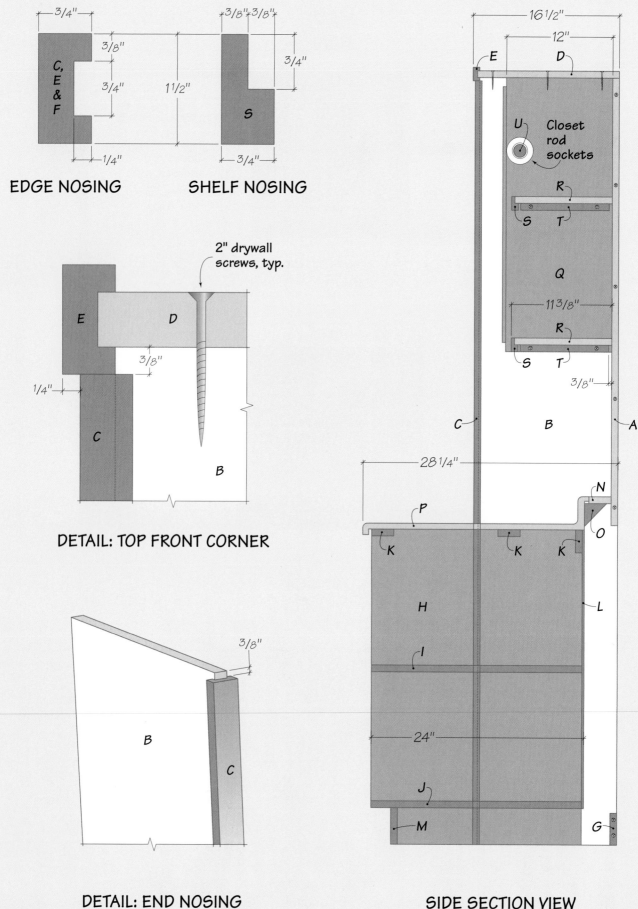

EDGE NOSING

SHELF NOSING

DETAIL: TOP FRONT CORNER

2" drywall screws, typ.

DETAIL: END NOSING

SIDE SECTION VIEW

Closet rod sockets

ing edges of the cabinet sides, bottom, shelf and front stretcher to cover the plywood edges.

23 Finish the cabinet. Fill the nailheads in the toe board with wood putty. Sand all surfaces and edges smooth, and topcoat with polyurethane.

24 Attach the countertop. Set the top in place, and attach it with 1¼-in. drywall screws driven up through the stretchers **(See Photo I)**.

BUILD & ATTACH THE LEDGE

25 Cut the melamine ledge to size. The purpose of this ledge is to make the front edge of the countertop align with the fronts of your washer and dryer. Adjust the width as needed to match the depth of your appliances. Cut matching biscuit slots in the front edge of the ledge and the top edge of the backsplash, positioning the slots so the surface of the ledge will be even with, or slightly below, the top of the backsplash.

26 Make the four ledge braces, and attach the ledge and braces to the countertop. Spread glue in the biscuit slots and on the mating surfaces of the ledge and splash. Insert the biscuits, and clamp the ledge in place against the splash. Once the glue dries, apply glue to the edges of the braces that fit against the backsplash and ledge, and clamp the braces in position **(See Photo J)**. Reinforce the braces with countersunk screws, if you wish, driving them into the backsplash. Be careful not to overdrive the screws so they pierce through the laminate.

INSTALL THE BASE CABINET

27 Set the the base cabinet in place below the upper cabinet. You can anchor the cabinet to the floor if you like, but this is optional. To do so, draw lines on the floor along both sides. Remove the cabinet, cut two 2 × 4 × 20-in. cleats, and fasten the cleats to the floor ¾ in. inside both reference lines. Reposition the cabinet over the cleats. Secure the cabinet with screws driven through the cabinet sides into the cleats.

28 We attached an under-cabinet light fixture to the bottom of the upper cabinet to serve as task lighting. This lighting is optional.

29 Move the appliances into position, and make your water, drain, electrical and venting connections.

PHOTO I: To attach the post-formed countertop, position it on the cabinet and drive 1¼-in. screws up through pilot holes in the stretchers.

PHOTO J: Use biscuits to align the ledge with the top edge of the backsplash, then glue and clamp this joint. After the glue sets, glue and clamp triangular ledge braces beneath the ledge. Reinforce the braces with screws.

Contemporary Basement Bar

This handsome dry bar with its laminate serving counter has lots of style, yet it is surprisingly easy to build. Behind its structure of asymmetrical curves are stock prefabricated base cabinets, eliminating the need for building doors, drawers and face frames. Add a post-formed laminate countertop to the cabinets, and you'll have a lower work counter to keep glassware and dishes out of sight. A welcome addition to any basement, den or family room, the bar functions equally well for formal cocktail parties or Monday night football fests.

Vital statistics

TYPE: Serving bar

OVERALL SIZE: 65L by 42H by 38D

MATERIAL: Red oak plywood and lumber, treated lumber, fir plywood, particleboard, plastic laminate, pre-fabricated bathroom vanity cabinets, post-formed countertop (for cabinets)

JOINERY: Butt joints reinforced with glue and screws or biscuits

CONSTRUCTION DETAILS:
- Front and end faces kerf-bent to wrap around curved plywood frame
- Face panels and front corner pieces attach with biscuit joints
- Sub-top and edging beneath serving counter are cut from one piece of plywood in order to fit together and register countertop on base

FINISH: Stain and polyurethane on oak parts

Building time

PREPARING STOCK: 1-2 hours

LAYOUT: 2-4 hours

CUTTING PARTS: 2-4 hours

ASSEMBLY: 2-4 hours

FINISHING: 2-4 hours

COUNTERTOP: 2-4 hours

INSTALLATION: 2-4 hours

TOTAL: 13-26 hours

Shopping List

- ☐ (1) 2 × 6 in. × 8 ft. treated lumber
- ☐ (2) ¾ in. × 4 × 8 ft. fir plywood
- ☐ (2) ¾ in. × 4 × 8 ft. red oak plywood
- ☐ (1) ¾ in. × 4 × 8 ft. particleboard
- ☐ (1) ¾ × 1½ in. × 8 ft. red oak
- ☐ (1) Plastic laminate (42 × 66 in. minimum, without edging)
- ☐ Laminate edging (1¾ in. × 20 lin. ft., or cut from a larger sheet)
- ☐ (1) 30-in. vanity base cabinet
- ☐ (1) 18-in. vanity base cabinet
- ☐ 48-in. post-formed vanity countertop
- ☐ Drywall screws (3-, 2½-, 2-, 1½-, 1¼-in.)
- ☐ Self-tapping masonry screws (3-in.)
- ☐ #20 biscuits, wood glue
- ☐ Construction adhesive, contact cement
- ☐ Finishing materials

Contemporary Basement Bar

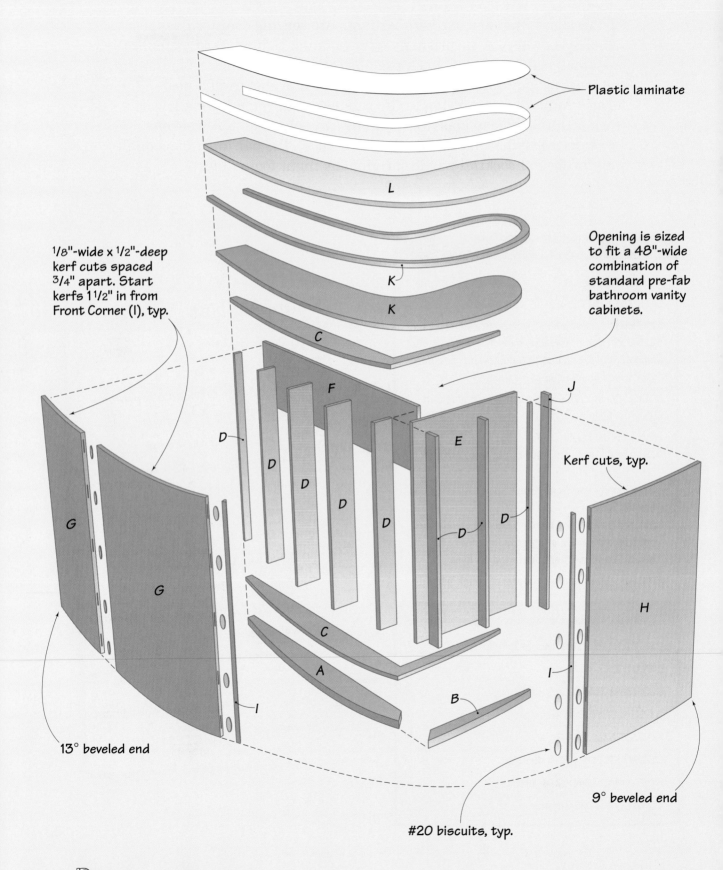

Plastic laminate

Opening is sized to fit a 48"-wide combination of standard pre-fab bathroom vanity cabinets.

1/8"-wide x 1/2"-deep kerf cuts spaced 3/4" apart. Start kerfs 1 1/2" in from Front Corner (I), typ.

Kerf cuts, typ.

13° beveled end

9° beveled end

#20 biscuits, typ.

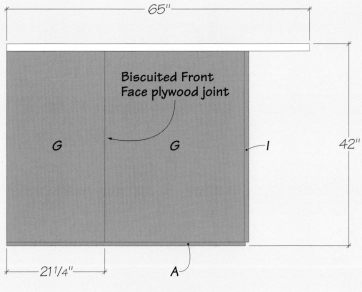

FRONT VIEW

65"

Biscuited Front
Face plywood joint

G   G   I

42"

21¼"   A

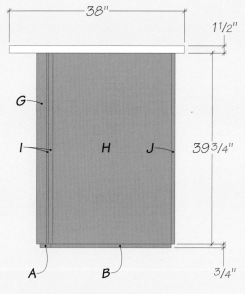

FINISHED-END VIEW

38"   1½"

G

I   H   J   39¾"

A   B   ¾"

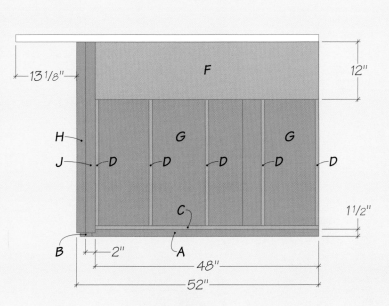

BACK VIEW

13⅛"

F   12"

H
J   D   G   D   G   D

C   1½"
B   2"   A

48"
52"

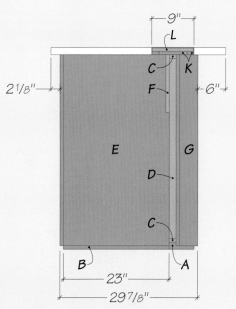

WALL-END VIEW

9"
L
C   K
21⅛"   F   6"

E   G

D

C

B   A
23"
29⅞"

Contemporary Basement Bar Cutting List

Part	No.	Size	Material
BASE			
A. Front mounting plate	1	1½ × 5⅜ × 51¼ in.	Treated lumber
B. End mounting plate	1	1½ × 2½ × 25½ in.	"
C. Top/bottom plates	2	¾ × 28⅜ × 51¼ in.	Fir plywood
D. Struts	8	¾ × varies × 37½ in.	"
E. End panel	1	¾ × 23 × 39¾ in.	Oak plywood
F. Splash panel	1	¾ × 48 × 12 in.	"

Part	No.	Size	Material
G. Front face	1	¾ × 51½+/- × 39¾ in.	Oak plywood
H. End face	1	¾ × 25¼+/- × 39¾ in.	"
I. Front corner	2	¾ × 1 × 39¾ in.	Oak
J. End cap	1	¾ × 2 × 39¾ in.	"
COUNTERTOP			
K. Sub-top/edging	1	¾ × 38 × 65 in.	Fir plywood
L. Top	1	¾ × 38 × 65 in.	Particleboard

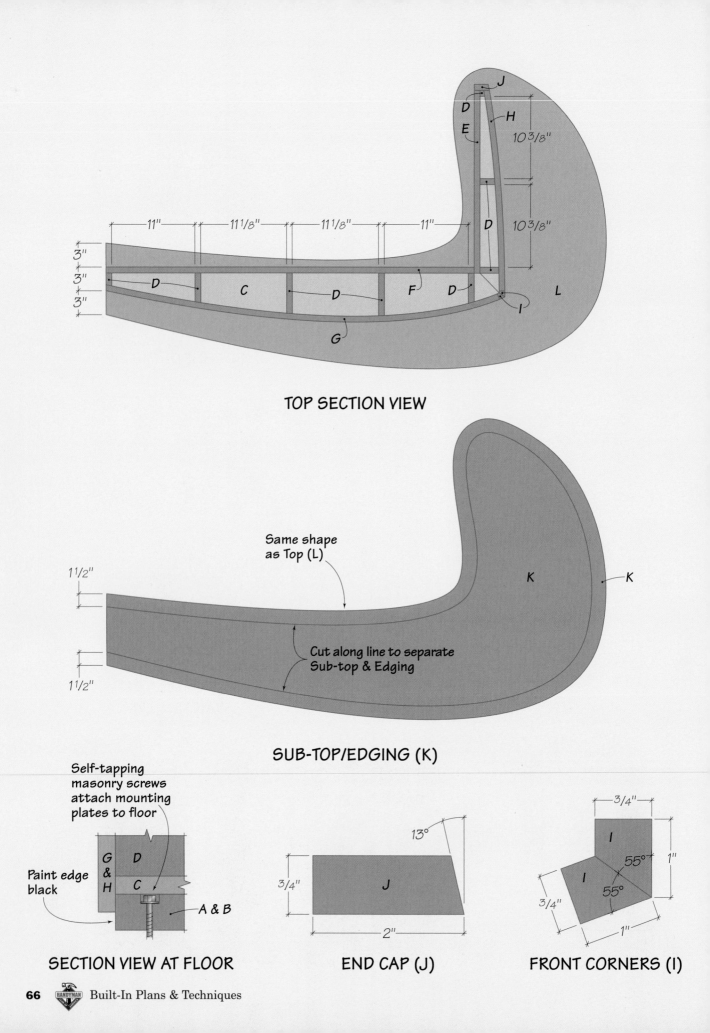

TOP SECTION VIEW

Same shape
as Top (L)

1 1/2"

1 1/2"

Cut along line to separate
Sub-top & Edging

K   K

SUB-TOP/EDGING (K)

Self-tapping
masonry screws
attach mounting
plates to floor

Paint edge
black

G
&
H

D

C

A & B

SECTION VIEW AT FLOOR

13°

3/4"

J

2"

END CAP (J)

3/4"

I

55°

55°

I

3/4"

1"

1"

FRONT CORNERS (I)

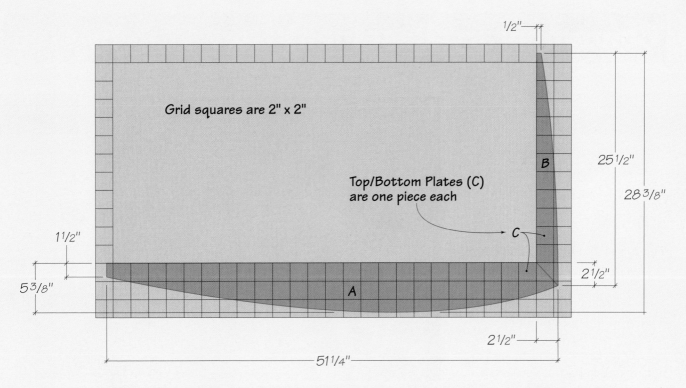

Grid squares are 2" x 2"

Top/Bottom Plates (C) are one piece each

1/2"

25 1/2"

28 3/8"

1 1/2"

5 3/8"

2 1/2"

2 1/2"

51 1/4"

A

B

C

LAYOUT: MOUNTING PLATES (A & B) & TOP/BOTTOM PLATES (C)

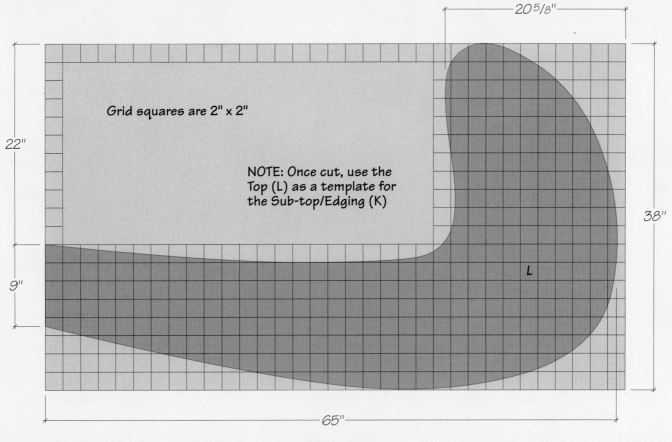

Grid squares are 2" x 2"

NOTE: Once cut, use the Top (L) as a template for the Sub-top/Edging (K)

20 5/8"

22"

9"

38"

65"

L

LAYOUT: TOP (L)

Contemporary Basement Bar **67**

The complete project is made up of four components: the bar base, serving counter, cabinets and the work top. This project is readily adaptable to suit your unique needs. If you have access to plumbing, make one of the cabinets a sink base and you've got a wet bar. If you want to store cool drinks, substitute an under-counter refrigerator for one of the cabinets. If you have the space for a full-fledged bar, install matching cabinets along the back wall, add a refrigerator, and use this plan as the front bar.

BUILD THE BASE

The bar base consists of a support structure clad with kerf-bent plywood "skin." Build the internal base structure first.

❶ Crosscut blanks for the front and end mounting plates, generously long, from treated lumber. Miter-cut a 45° angle at one end of each blank.

❷ Mark the profiles and cut the mounting plates to shape. Using the grid drawing shown on the top of page 67, transfer the curved profiles to the blanks. Tap finish nails at two or three reference points along each blank. Bend a thin wood or hardboard batten strip to conform to the curvature established by the nails, and trace

PHOTO A: Use a flexible wood batten held in place with a few finish nails to draw smooth curved profiles onto the mounting plate blanks. Cut the curves with a jig saw. Notice that the mounting plates meet at a 45° angle at the front corner.

PHOTO B: Trace two patterns of the mounting plates set together on a piece of ¾-in. plywood to form the top and bottom plates.

the shapes (**See Photo A**). Cut along your layout lines with a jig saw. Sand the cuts smooth. Measure along the inside straight edges of the workpieces, and cut the plates to final length.

❸ Cut the top and bottom plates

to size and shape: Set the mounting plates together on ¾-in. fir plywood and outline two identical shapes, forming the top and bottom plates (**See Photo B**). Cut out these plywood parts.

❹ Measure and mark the posi-

PHOTO C: Glue and clamp the vertical struts between the top and bottom plates to form the base structure. Drive 1½-in. drywall screws through the plates and into the struts to reinforce these joints.

PHOTO D: Lay out the two front corner strips on an oak blank so the beveled edges of the corner strips face inward. Mark and cut biscuit slots along both edges of the blank to match the slots you cut in the plywood face panels. Then bevel-rip the corner pieces from the blank.

tions of the struts on the bottom and top plates, using the *Top Section View* drawing, page 66, for determining strut spacing. Draw the strut layout lines with a square held against the flat inside edges of the workpieces.

5 Confirm the actual width of each strut (the widths will vary), and cut them to size from ¾-in. plywood.

6 Build the base. Drill countersunk pilot holes through the bottom and top plates at the strut locations. Apply glue to the ends of the struts, clamp them in place between the plates and fasten with 1½-in. drywall screws **(See Photo C)**.

MAKE & ATTACH THE FACING

The outer "skin" that wraps around the bar base consists of three panels of plywood joined at the front corner of the base to two narrow strips of oak. We'll employ a cabinetmaker's technique called "kerf-bending" to bend the plywood around the curved base. This process involves cutting a series of closely spaced shallow saw kerfs top to bottom into the back faces of the plywood, allowing the plywood to flex.

7 Cut the front and end faces to size from oak plywood, leaving a little extra length (left-to-right) for final fitting to the wall and end cap. Since the grain pattern on the front face runs vertically, and the front face is wider than 48 in., you'll build it from

two pieces of plywood butted together on-edge and joined with biscuits and glue. Lay out and cut #20 biscuit slots along the mating edges of the front face pieces. Glue and clamp them together.

8 Cut #20 biscuit slots in the edges of the front and end faces that will be joined to the oak front corner pieces.

9 Make the corner pieces. Start with a strip of oak lumber, 3 in. wide by 39¾ in. long, which you'll rip to make the final corner pieces. Lay out the two beveled

PHOTO E: Cut biscuit joints into the beveled edges of both front corner pieces. Glue and clamp the oak pieces together with biscuits installed. Spring clamps are a good choice for holding the bevel joint closed, but rubber bands or masking tape also would work.

PHOTO F: Use a kerf-cutting jig and a circular saw to cut ½-in.-deep kerfs into the backs of the plywood face panels. The leading edge of the jig indexes where the blade will cut. These kerf cuts will allow the plywood to bend around the curved base shape.

PHOTO G: Fasten the face assembly to the base with glue and finish nails. Start at the front corner, nailing down the face panels outward to the ends of the base. If you start at one of the ends of the base first, the front corner may not align properly with the front corner of the base. Once the face assembly is secured, trim away any facing that overhangs the base ends.

front corner pieces on the blank, using the *Front Corners* drawing, page 66, as a guide. Clamp this blank to your worksurface. Mark biscuit locations along both long edges of the blank to match the ones you cut into the mating edges of the front and end faces. Cut #20 biscuit slots at these locations (**See Photo D**).

⑩ Bevel-rip the front corner pieces to size on the table saw.

⑪ Build the front corner. Cut slots for #20 biscuits in the mating beveled edges of the corner pieces. Spread glue into the biscuit slots and along the beveled edges, and clamp the corner pieces together (**See Photo E**).

⑫ Cut a series of ½-in.-deep kerfs into the backs of the front and end face panels with your circular saw and a kerf-cutting jig (See *Kerf-Cutting Jig,* below). Orient the cuts so they'll run vertically when these face panels are installed. Inset the first kerfs

Kerf-cutting jig

An efficient method for kerf-cutting the plywood facing in this project is to build a simple jig for your circular saw. Start with a 40-in.-long piece of ¼-in. hardboard about 12 to 14 in. wide. Fasten a strip of ¾-in. plywood about 3 in. wide and 40 in. long along one edge of the hardboard. Set your circular saw on the hardboard and against the plywood strip and trim the hardboard using the plywood as a straightedge. Now the edge of the hardboard aligns exactly with your saw blade and becomes an easy reference line for indexing your kerf cuts.

1½ in. from the edges that will fasten to the front corner. Space the kerfs ¾ in. apart (**See Photo F**).

⓭ Attach the front face to the front corner with biscuits and glue, stretching wide masking tape across the joint to hold it closed until the glue dries. Fasten the end face to the front corner in the same fashion to complete the face assembly.

⓮ Fasten the face assembly to the bar base. Position the face assembly on the base frame, with the corner snug, the top edges flush and the bottom edge overhanging the bottom of the base by ¾ in. Attach the face assembly to the base with glue and finish nails starting at the front corner and moving out toward the ends (**See Photo G**).

⓯ Mark and trim the ends of the face assembly flush with the ends of the base. NOTE: *This can be done either by marking the angles and trimming with a circular saw or by sanding the edges flush with a belt sander.* Be careful to keep the ends of the faces aligned with the ends of the base so the joints at the end cap and wall will be tight and clean.

COMPLETE THE BASE

⓰ Cut the end panel and cap to size, and attach them to the base. Fasten the end panel first, using glue and finish nails along the top edge and screws in the portion that will be hidden by the cabinet. Attach the end cap with glue and finish nails. Sand the outer long edge of the end cap to match the overall curved profile of the end face (about 13°).

⓱ Cut the splash panel to size and attach it with glue, finish nails and screws.

⓲ Fill the nail and screw holes in the base, and sand the surfaces and edges smooth. Apply your choice of stain, followed by several coats of polyurethane.

INSTALL THE BASE

⓳ Paint the edges of the mounting plates black to help minimize their appearance when the project is installed.

⓴ Position and install the mounting plates. The end plate should be positioned with a clearance of 42 in. from the back wall or any other fixed structure. Use shims to level the plates if necessary, and make sure the corner joint created by the mounting plates is tight. Drill countersunk pilot holes, and fasten the

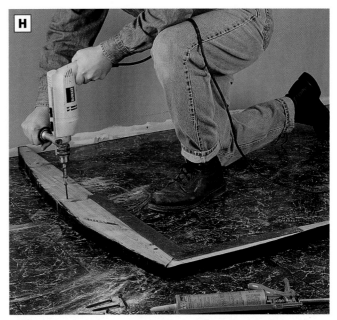

PHOTO H: Position the mounting plates on the floor, mark their locations and lay a bead of construction adhesive in the installation area. Drill pilot holes through the mounting plates for the installation screws. Set the plates in place and secure them to the floor with self-tapping masonry screws (if your floor is made of concrete). You'll need to drill pilot holes into the floor for the masonry screws first, with a hammer drill and masonry bit.

PHOTO I: Set the base in place on the mounting plates. Fasten the base to the mounting plates with screws driven through the bottom plate. We added a scrap plywood strip to the inside edge of the front mounting plate to serve as a cabinet spacer later.

PHOTO J: Make a grid with 2 × 2-in. squares on a sheet of particleboard, and plot points for the top panel on the grid, using the *Layout: Top* drawing, page 67, as a guide. Drive finish nails at several of these reference points and bend a flexible batten around the nails to form smooth layout lines. Draw the countertop shape by tracing along the batten. Remove the nails.

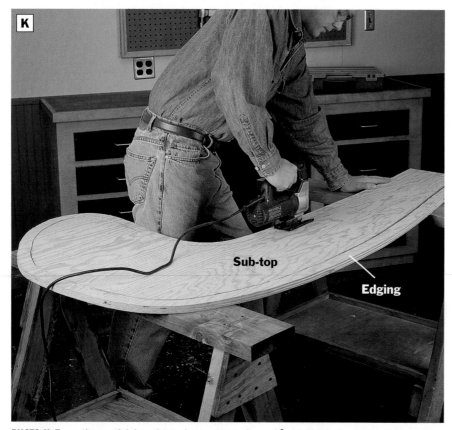

PHOTO K: Trace the particleboard top shape onto a piece of ¾-in. plywood, and use a compass to scribe a line around the top, inset 1½ in. from the edge. You've now formed both the sub-top and edging. Separate these workpieces by cutting along your layout line with a jig saw.

plates to the floor with panel adhesive and 3-in. self-tapping masonry screws (**See Photo H**). In concrete floors, bore pilot holes for the screws with a masonry bit and hammer drill.

㉑ Attach a ¾ × 3-in. strip of scrap plywood along the inside edge of the front mounting plate. This piece matches the thickness of the splash panel and serves as a spacer for cabinet installation.

㉒ Stand the base in position on the mounting plates. Make sure the top of the structure is level both ways. Shim as needed. Install the base by driving 1½-in. drywall screws through the bottom base plate into the mounting plates (**See Photo I**).

BUILD & INSTALL THE SERVING COUNTER

The serving counter consists of a particleboard top that rests on a plywood sub-top fastened to the bar base. The sub-top fits inside a strip of plywood edging that wraps around the particleboard top. You'll use the top as a template for drawing the sub-top/edging shape on one piece of plywood, then cut out both of these parts. The sub-top and edging pieces serve several purposes: they build up the thickness of the countertop as well as register and attach it to the base.

㉓ Lay out the top. The top is made of particleboard, which provides a stable backing for plastic laminate. Refer to the *Layout: Top* grid drawing, page 67, to draw the grid onto particleboard. Use a long flexible wood batten bent around finish nails tacked to the particleboard to help draw smooth curves (**See Photo J**), and cut out the top with a jig saw.

24 Use the top as a pattern for tracing the plywood sub-top/edging workpiece onto ¾-in. plywood. Cut along your layout line with a jig saw to form the sub-top/edging workpiece.

25 Scribe a line parallel to the outer edge of the sub-top/edging workpiece (except where it meets the wall) and 1½ in. inside it to form the edging. TIP: *A compass set to 1½ in. makes this task easy. Let the compass point follow the outer edge of the workpiece so the pencil draws the sub-top cutting line.* Cut along the line with a jig saw to separate the edging from the sub-top **(See Photo K)**.

26 Attach the plywood edging to the particleboard top with glue and nails. Be careful to attach the edging to the correct face of the top—the edging faces down once the countertop is installed. The edges of the parts should be flush. Sand until this built-up edge is smooth all around.

27 Apply 1½-in.-wide strips of laminate edging around the built-up edge of the top, using contact cement. You should spread a layer of cement onto both the laminate and the built-up edge. Plan the edging installation so any joints fall in places where the curves are gradual. When the cement is dry, firmly press the laminate in place **(See Photo L)**, starting at one end. Pass a J-roller over the edging to ensure good adhesion.

28 Trim away any edging overhang with a router and piloted laminate-trimming bit **(See Photo M)**. Complete the trimming with a file held flat against the surface of the particleboard. File off any remaining sharp corners as well.

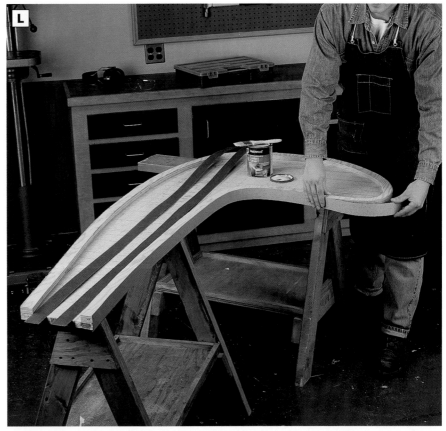

PHOTO L: Spread contact cement onto the backs of the plastic laminate edging as well as the built-up edges of the countertop. When the adhesive is dry, press the edging in place. Locate seams in the edging where the curves are most gradual.

PHOTO M: Trim the laminate edging flush with the top and bottom surfaces of the countertop using a router and piloted laminate-trimming bit. File the edging as needed so it is perfectly flush with the top surface of the counter.

PHOTO N: Glue down a sheet of plastic laminate to cover the top face of the countertop, spreading contact cement over both the laminate and the particleboard. To make positioning the laminate easier and more foolproof, lay spacer strips over the particleboard first, set the laminate in place, and pull out the strips one at a time, starting from the center and working outward.

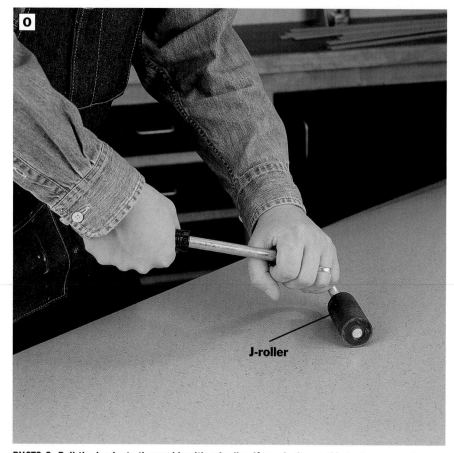

J-roller

PHOTO O: Roll the laminate thoroughly with a J-roller. If you don't own this tool, you can also use a towel wrapped around a length of 2 × 4, rubbing firmly from the center out toward the edges.

㉙ Attach the plastic laminate to the top. Spread even layers of contact cement on the particleboard top and the back face of the laminate sheet. When the cement is dry, place thin scrap spacer strips across the top, held 6 to 8 in. apart. Lay the laminate sheet in place on the spacer strips. Beginning at the middle and working outward in both directions, apply the laminate to the top by pulling the spacers out one at a time (See Photo N), and press the laminate firmly in place.

㉚ After all the spacers are removed, roll the laminate surface thoroughly with a J-roller (See Photo O), starting at the center and working toward the edges.

㉛ Trim the laminate top flush with the laminate edging, using a router and flush-trimming bit.

㉜ Install the sub-top. First, test-fit the sub-top inside the countertop edging. If the sub-top fits too snugly, belt-sand the edges of the sub-top to relax the fit. Then slip the sub-top back in place in the countertop, and set the countertop assembly on the bar base. Position the countertop, using the *Top Section View* drawing, page 66, as a guide. Carefully lift off the countertop without shifting the sub-top on the base. Attach the sub-top to the top plate of the base with countersunk 1½-in. drywall screws (See Photo P).

㉝ Install the countertop. Drill countersunk pilot holes from underneath the sub-top where it overhangs the base. Set the countertop in place on the sub-top and drive 1¼-in. drywall screws up through the sub-top from below to fasten the countertop.

INSTALL THE CABINETS

This project uses prefabricated vanity-sized base cabinets because they are shorter and shallower than kitchen base cabinets. The lower worksurface these cabinets provide allows for setting glassware and serving pieces on the work counter while keeping them out of view behind the bar. Some manufacturers install backs on these cabinets, others do not.

34 If your cabinets do not come with backs, consider making them from hardboard to prevent the contents of the cabinets from falling inside the bar base later. Or, extend the plywood splash panel to the floor.

35 Install the cabinets. Fasten them together with their front faces aligned, driving screws through the cabinet sides. Slide the cabinets in place and level them on the floor with shims, if necessary. Screw through the cabinet hang strips into the backsplash **(See Photo Q)**.

ADD THE WORK TOP

This project was designed to accept a standard 48-in. length of post-formed vanity top with a low backsplash. It is not necessary for the laminate patterns to be the same between the two tops. You might choose a bold color or pattern for the serving counter and a quieter, complementary color or pattern for the work top.

36 If necessary, attach cleats to the inside top edges of the cabinet ends, and install the work top with screws driven up from inside the cabinets.

PHOTO P: Locate the sub-top on the base structure and fasten it to the top plate with drywall screws. Set the countertop in place first to help position the sub-base. Once you've attached the sub-top, set the countertop back in place and drive screws up through the sub-top.

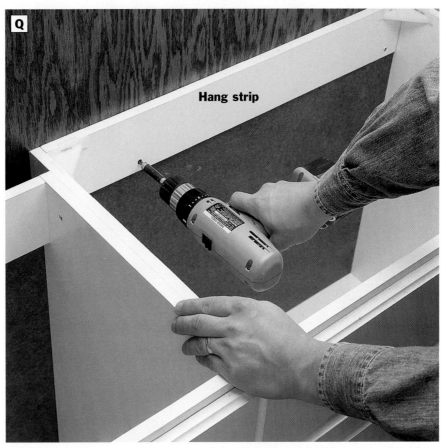

Hang strip

PHOTO Q: Fasten the base cabinets together with screws driven through the cabinet sides, then attach the cabinets to the backsplash by driving screws through the cabinet hang strips.

Floor-to-Ceiling Bookcase

With its fluted stiles and shaped cornice blocks, this floor-to-ceiling mahogany bookcase will add a touch of sophistication and elegance to any room. The rich tones of Honduras mahogany evoke memories of serious libraries with their ambiance of good books, warm wood, soft light and maybe even a whiff of leather in the air. Designed to be easily adaptable, it is a simple matter to expand or reduce the size of this bookcase by adding or subtracting one or more of the cabinet boxes. The project is even ready for you to add brackets and a rolling library ladder if you should so choose.

Vital statistics

TYPE: Bookcase

OVERALL SIZE: 75L by 96H by 14½D

MATERIAL: Honduras mahogany plywood and lumber

JOINERY: Butt joints reinforced with glue and screws or dowels

CONSTRUCTION DETAILS:
· Three cabinet box sizes match, making the process of cutting parts more efficient
· Flutes on the face frame stiles are milled with a router, core box bit and shop-made jig
· Cornice block beaded profiles are gang-routed on a shop-made jig
· Finished end is scribed along its rabbeted back edge so the project fits tight to the wall

FINISH: Stain and polyurethane

Building time

PREPARING STOCK: 4-6 hours

LAYOUT: 1-2 hours

CUTTING PARTS: 4-6 hours

ASSEMBLY: 2-4 hours

FINISHING: 2-4 hours

INSTALLATION: 2-4 hours

TOTAL: 15-26 hours

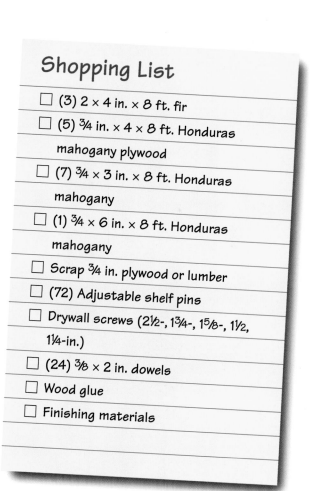

Shopping List

☐ (3) 2 × 4 in. × 8 ft. fir

☐ (5) ¾ in. × 4 × 8 ft. Honduras mahogany plywood

☐ (7) ¾ × 3 in. × 8 ft. Honduras mahogany

☐ (1) ¾ × 6 in. × 8 ft. Honduras mahogany

☐ Scrap ¾ in. plywood or lumber

☐ (72) Adjustable shelf pins

☐ Drywall screws (2½-, 1¾-, 1⅝-, 1½, 1¼-in.)

☐ (24) ⅜ × 2 in. dowels

☐ Wood glue

☐ Finishing materials

Floor-to-Ceiling Bookcase

Match to your room's moldings

45° mitered ends

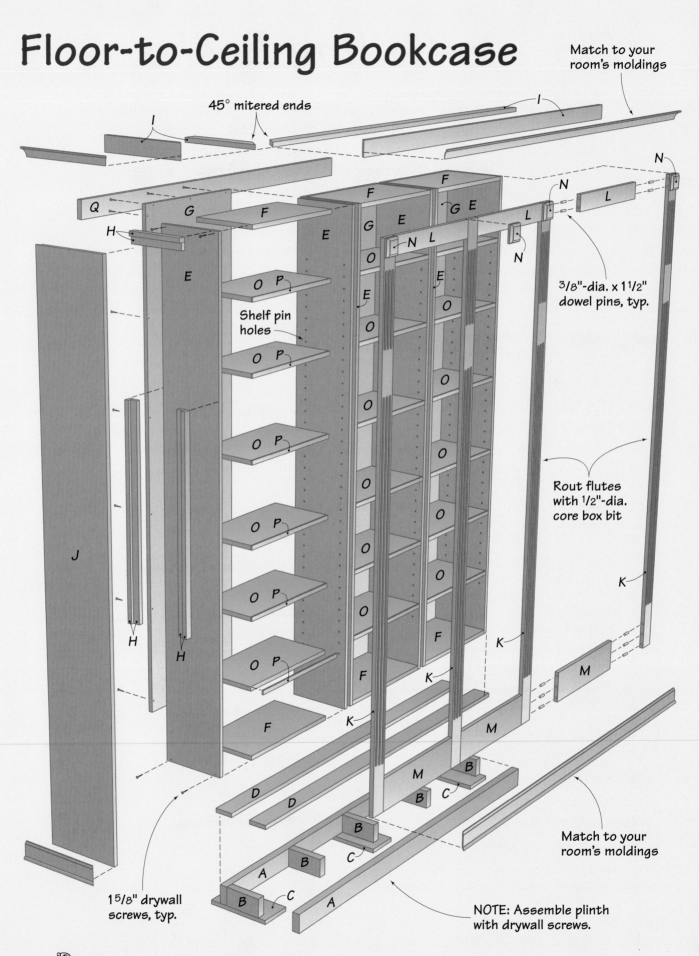

Shelf pin holes

$3/8"$-dia. x $1\frac{1}{2}"$ dowel pins, typ.

Rout flutes with $1/2"$-dia. core box bit

$1\frac{5}{8}"$ drywall screws, typ.

Match to your room's moldings

NOTE: Assemble plinth with drywall screws.

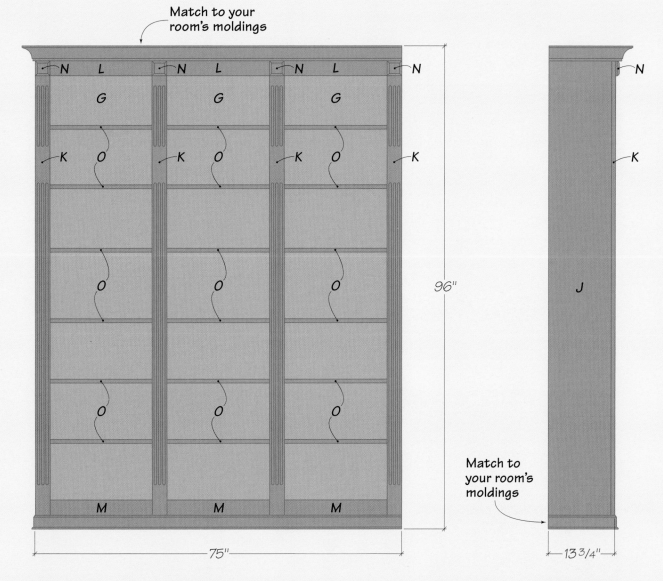

FRONT VIEW

SIDE VIEW

Floor-to-Ceiling Bookcase Cutting List

Part	No.	Size	Material
A. Plinth stretchers	2	1½ × 3½ × 74¼ in.	Fir
B. Plinth struts	5	1½ × 3½ × 7¼ in.	"
C. Plinth cleats	3	¾ × 6 × 12¼ in.	Fir plywood
D. Plinth strips	2	¾ × 3 × 74¼ in.	"
E. Box sides	6	¾ × 11½ × 88 in.	Mahogany plywood
F. Box tops/ bottoms	6	¾ × 11½ × 21½ in.	"
G. Box backs	3	¾ × 23 × 88 in.	"
H. End spacer strips	2	¾ × 1¼ in. × 8 lin. ft.	Fir plywood
I. Crown backer strips	2	¾ × 2½ in. × 8 lin. ft.	Mahogany
J. Finished end	1	¾ × 13 × 93 in.	Mahogany plywood
K. Face frame stiles	4	¾ × 3 × 93 in.	Mahogany
L. Face frame top rails	3	¾ × 3 × 21 in.	"
M. Face frame bottom rails	3	¾ × 5¾ × 21 in.	"
N. Cornice blocks	4	¾ × 3 × 3 in.	"
O. Shelves	18	¾ × 11¼ × 21¼ in.	Mahogany plywood
P. Shelf edging	18	¼ × ¾ × 21¼ in.	Mahogany
Q. Wall spacer	1	¾ × 3½ × 74 in.	Fir plywood

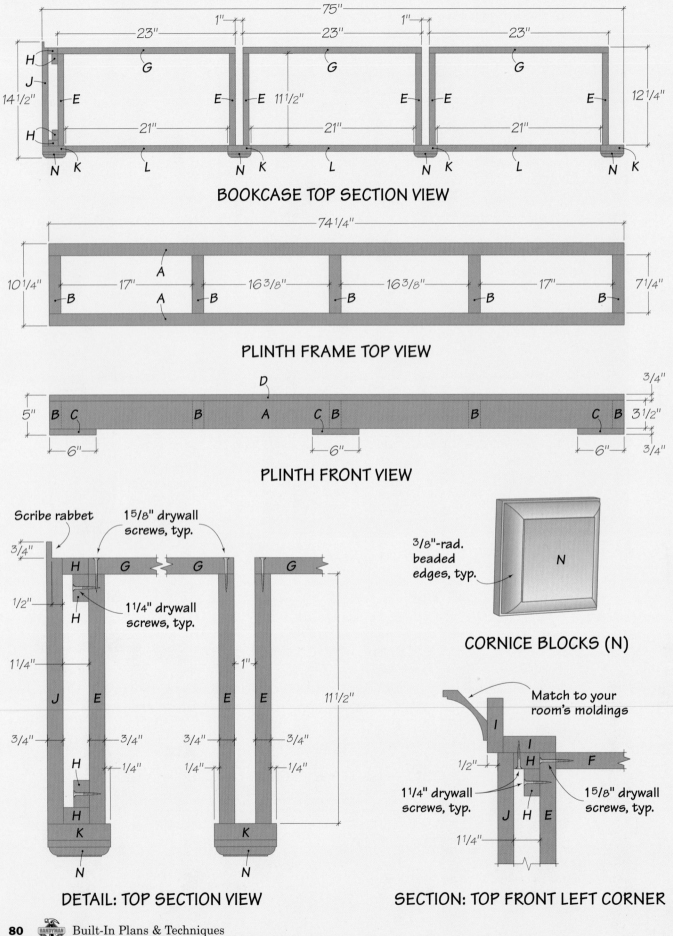

BOOKCASE TOP SECTION VIEW

PLINTH FRAME TOP VIEW

PLINTH FRONT VIEW

Scribe rabbet

1⁵/₈" drywall screws, typ.

1¹/₄" drywall screws, typ.

3/8"-rad. beaded edges, typ.

CORNICE BLOCKS (N)

Match to your room's moldings

1¹/₄" drywall screws, typ.

1⁵/₈" drywall screws, typ.

DETAIL: TOP SECTION VIEW

SECTION: TOP FRONT LEFT CORNER

the joints, insert the glued dowels and clamp the frames together **(See Photo H)**.

14 Complete assembly of the face frame at the installation site. Glue and clamp the center top and bottom rails *(See Photo J)* in place between the outer frames with dowels installed in the joints.

15 Make the cornice blocks. First, rip and crosscut the four cornice blocks to size. The cornices receive a ⅜-in. beaded profile around all four outer edges, but they are too small to rout safely one at a time on a router pad. A safer and faster method is to make a jig that holds and aligns all four cornices so you can gang-rout one edge of the cornices in one pass. Build the jig, set the cornices in place and make four successive router passes, flipping the blocks a quarter turn to mill the four edges **(See Photo I)**.

16 Attach the cornices to the face frame with glue and 1¼-in. drywall screws, driven through the back of the face frame. Stain and varnish the face frame.

17 Install the face frame. Position the frame left-to-right against the cabinet boxes, and make sure the top edges of the lower rails are flush with the surfaces of the box bottoms. Shim the frame if necessary. Attach the frame to the front edges of the box with glue and finish nails **(See Photo J)**.

ATTACH THE CROWN ASSEMBLY

18 Cut the crown backer strips to size and join them together with glue and nails or screws as shown in the *Side Section View,* page 81. The backer overhangs the cabinet end and the face of the cornice blocks by ½ in. Measure and cut lengths of backer for the bookcase front and exposed end. Miter-cut the adjoining ends of the backer sections at 45°. Fasten the sections together before installation.

19 Set the crown backers in place and install with 1¼-in. drywall screws driven up through the cabinet tops and end spacers **(See Photo K)**.

20 Conceal the gap between the top of the crown backer assembly and the ceiling with cove molding. Miter-cut and attach the cove to the backer strips with finish nails. Install base molding to match your room molding.

PHOTO J: Attach the frame with glue and nails. Make sure the top edges of the lower rails are flush with the bottoms of the boxes before you fasten the frame in place. Shim under the face frame if necessary.

PHOTO K: Install the crown backer assembly with screws driven through the cabinet box tops. To achieve a tight corner joint, fasten the sections together before installation. Then wrap the backer assembly with cove molding to hide the ceiling joint.

Window Seat with Shelving

This window seat really transforms a room! It provides ample storage, display space and a comfortable sunny spot for reading a book or sipping a cup of coffee—all in one attractive project. Because built-in units like this can sometimes overwhelm a small room, we painted our window seat white to keep it light and bright. This beautiful and functional project is simplified by using stock-sized, pre-made cabinet doors. You'll be surprised how quickly you can go from imagining how nice a window seat would be, to actually enjoying this piece of furniture in your home.

Vital statistics

TYPE: Window seat

OVERALL SIZE: 115¾L by 84⅝H by 20¾D

MATERIAL: Birch plywood and lumber, fir plywood, pine, stock overlay doors

JOINERY: Dado and rabbet joints reinforced with glue and screws or nails; biscuit joints

CONSTRUCTION DETAILS:
- Upper cabinet tops, bottoms and backs fit into dadoes and rabbets in the cabinet ends
- Shelves are reinforced with birch nosing along the front edge
- Shelves are hung on metal shelf standards mortised into dadoes in the cabinet ends
- Doors are purchased pre-assembled for ease of construction

FINISH: Primer and paint

Building time

PREPARING STOCK: 1-2 hours

LAYOUT: 3-4 hours

CUTTING PARTS: 2-4 hours

ASSEMBLY: 4-6 hours

FINISHING: 6-8 hours

INSTALLATION: 6-8 hours

TOTAL: 22-32 hours

Shopping List

- ☐ (1) ¾ in. × 4 × 8 ft. fir plywood
- ☐ (1) ¾ in. × 4 × 4 ft. fir plywood
- ☐ (1) ¼ in. × 4 × 8 ft. fir plywood (or hardboard)
- ☐ (3) ¾ in. × 4 × 8 ft. birch plywood
- ☐ (2) ½ in. × 4 × 8 ft. birch plywood
- ☐ (4) ¾ × 4 in. × 6 ft. birch
- ☐ (3) ¾ × 6 in. × 8 ft. birch
- ☐ (1) ¾ × 1½ in. × 10 ft. birch
- ☐ (4) ¾ × 2½ in. × 6 ft. pine
- ☐ 9/16 × 3¼ in. crown molding (12 lin. ft.)
- ☐ ½ × ½ in. quarter-round molding (12 lin. ft.)
- ☐ ½ × ½ in. base shoe molding (12 lin. ft.)
- ☐ (8) Overlay door (¾ × 13 × 13 in.)
- ☐ (8) White metal shelf standards (60 in.)
- ☐ (32) Shelf clips
- ☐ (16) Brass self-closing ½-in. overlay hinges
- ☐ (8) Door knobs
- ☐ Drywall screws (3-, 2½-, 1½-, 1¼-in.)
- ☐ #20 biscuits
- ☐ Wood glue
- ☐ Finishing materials

Window Seat with Shelving

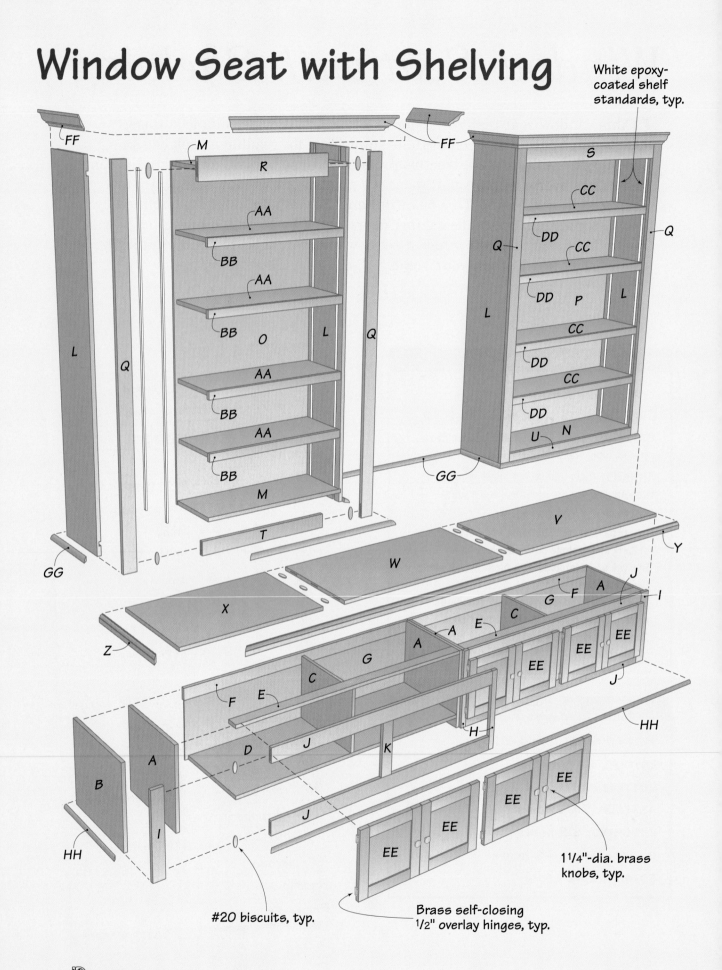

White epoxy-coated shelf standards, typ.

FF

FF

FF

M

R

S

AA

CC

BB

Q

DD

Q

AA

CC

BB

DD

L

O

L

Q

P

L

AA

CC

BB

DD

AA

CC

L

BB

DD

M

U

N

GG

GG

V

Y

W

J

A

F

I

X

G

C

G

A

E

EE

J

Z

C

A

EE

EE

G

EE

F

E

J

D

H

HH

J

K

B

A

EE

EE

I

EE

EE

HH

#20 biscuits, typ.

Brass self-closing 1/2" overlay hinges, typ.

1 1/4"-dia. brass knobs, typ.

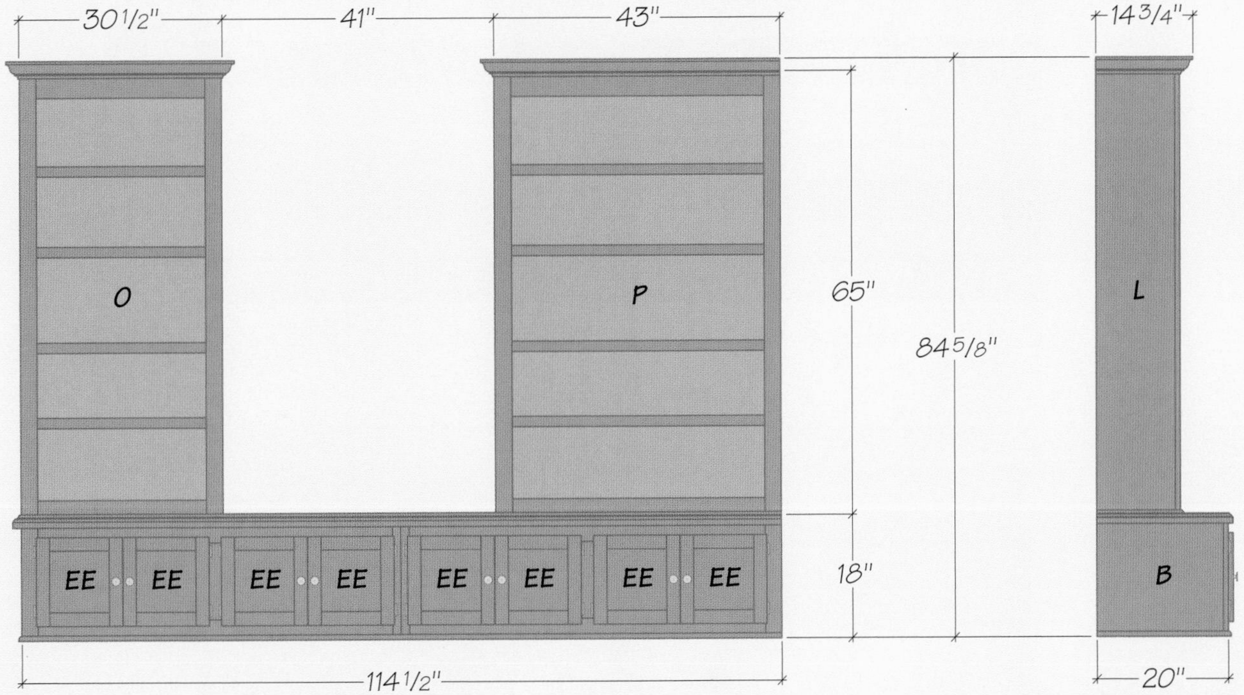

FRONT VIEW SIDE VIEW

Window Seat Cutting List

Part	No.	Size	Material
BASE CABINET PARTS			
A. Ends	4	¾ × 17¾ × 17¼ in.	Fir plywood
B. Finished end	1	¾ × 19¼ × 17¼ in.	Birch plywood
C. Dividers	2	¾ × 17¾ × 13½ in.	Fir plywood
D. Bottoms	2	¾ × 17¾ × 55 in.	"
E. Stretchers	2	¾ × 2½ × 55 in.	Pine
F. Hang strips	2	¾ × 2½ × 56½ in.	"
G. Backs	2	¼ × 12½ × 56½ in.	Fir plywood
BASE FRAME PARTS			
H. Center stiles	2	¾ × 1¼ × 17¼ in.	Birch
I. Outer stiles	2	¾ × 2½ × 17¼ in.	"
J. Rails	4	¾ × 3 × 53½ in.	"
K. Mullions	2	¾ × 2⅜ × 11¼ in.	"
UPPER CABINET PARTS			
L. Ends	4	¾ × 12 × 65 in.	Birch plywood
M. Left top, bottom	2	¾ × 11 × 29¾ in.	"
N. Right top, bottom	2	¾ × 11 × 41½ in.	"
O. Left back	1	½ × 30 × 60¾ in.	"
P. Right back	1	½ × 41¾ × 60¾ in.	"

Part	No.	Size	Material
UPPER FRAME PARTS			
Q. Stiles	4	¾ × 2½ × 65 in.	Birch
R. Left top rail	1	¾ × 3¾ × 25½ in.	"
S. Right top rail	1	¾ × 3¾ × 38 in.	"
T. Left bottom rail	1	¾ × 2½ × 25½ in.	"
U. Right bottom rail	1	¾ × 2½ × 38 in.	"
SEAT PARTS			
V. Seat section	1	¾ × 20 × 43 in.	Birch plywood
W. Seat section	1	¾ × 20 × 41 in.	"
X. Seat section	1	¾ × 20 × 31 in.	"
Y. Front nosing	1	¾ × 1½ × 115¾ in.	Birch
Z. End nosing	1	¾ × 1½ × 21 in.	"
REMAINING PARTS			
AA. Left shelves	4	¾ × 10 3/16 × 28⅞ in.	Birch plywood
BB. Nosing	4	¾ × 1½ × 28⅞ in.	Birch
CC. Right shelves	4	¾ × 10 3/16 × 40⅝ in.	Birch plywood
DD. Nosing	4	¾ × 1½ × 40⅝ in.	Birch
EE. Overlay doors	8	¾ × 13 × 13 in.	Pre-made
FF. Crown	1	9/16 × 3¼ in. × 12 lin. ft	Hardwood molding
GG. Quarter round	1	½ × ½ in. × 12 lin. ft	"
HH. Base shoe	1	½ × ½ in. × 12 lin. ft	"

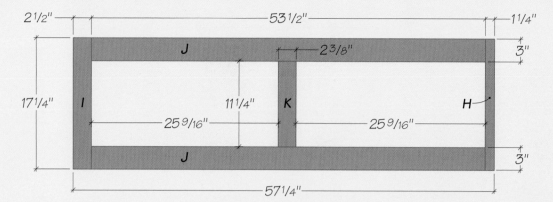

BASE FACE FRAMES

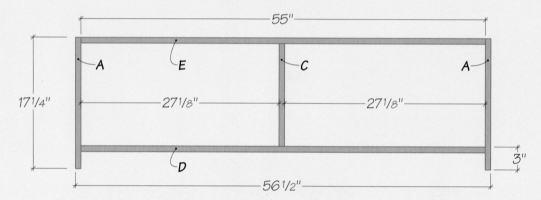

BASE CABINETS

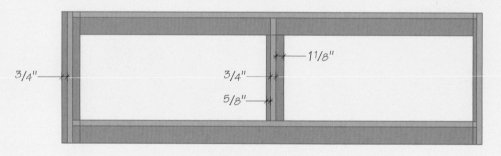

LEFT BASE FACE FRAME/CABINET

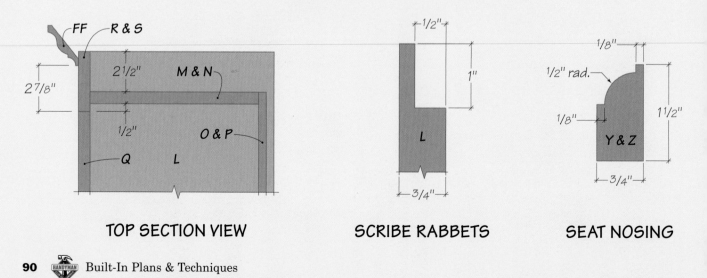

TOP SECTION VIEW　　　　**SCRIBE RABBETS**　　　　**SEAT NOSING**

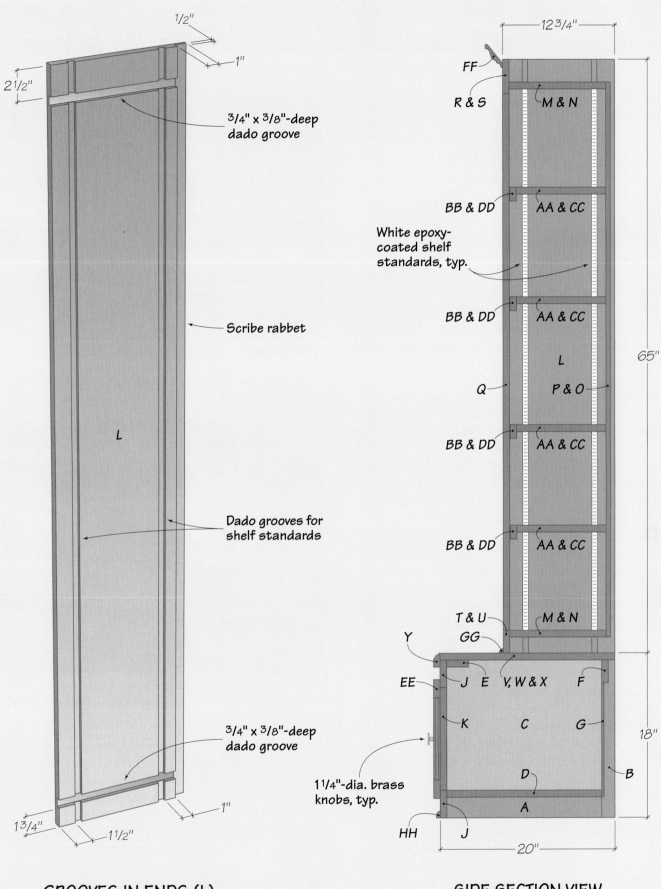

GROOVES IN ENDS (L)

1/2"

1"

2 1/2"

3/4" x 3/8"-deep
dado groove

Scribe rabbet

L

Dado grooves for
shelf standards

3/4" x 3/8"-deep
dado groove

1 3/4"

1 1/2"

1"

SIDE SECTION VIEW

12 3/4"

FF

R & S

M & N

BB & DD

AA & CC

White epoxy-
coated shelf
standards, typ.

BB & DD

AA & CC

L

Q

P & O

65"

BB & DD

AA & CC

BB & DD

AA & CC

T & U

M & N

GG

Y

J E V, W & X

F

EE

K

C

G

D

B

18"

1 1/4"-dia. brass
knobs, typ.

A

HH

J

20"

BUILD THE BASE CABINETS

The base storage unit of the window seat consists of two identical cabinets and two identical face frames. However, the frame for the left cabinet is applied with the wide stile on the left, and the frame for the right cabinet is flipped so the wide stile is on the right. The combined width of the narrow center stiles equals the wide outer stiles.

❶ Make the cabinet parts. Cut the four ends, two bottoms and two dividers to size from fir plywood. Rip and crosscut the stretchers and hang strips from pine lumber. Measure and mark the locations where the bottoms are joined to the ends and where the dividers are joined to the bottoms, hang strips and stretchers (See the *Base Cabinets* drawing, page 90).

❷ Build the base cabinets, one at a time. Spread glue on the ends of the bottom of the first cabinet, clamp it in place between the cabinet ends and attach the parts with countersunk 1½-in. drywall screws, driven through the ends. Clamp the stretcher in place between the ends so it is flush with the top front corners of the end panels. Fasten the ends to the stretcher with screws. Position and attach the divider with glue and screws, driven up through the bottom and down through the stretcher. Attach the hang strip to the back edges of the ends and divider with 1½-in. screws, holding its top edge flush with the top back corners of the ends. Follow the same procedure to assemble the other base cabinet **(See Photo A)**.

❸ Make and attach the cabinet backs. The backs on these cabinets function as dust covers, rather than structural components. Cut the two back panels to size from ¼-in. plywood. Attach the backs to the cabinet boxes with staples or screws. The backs will overlap the cabinet ends and bottoms but fit snug against the bottom edges of the hang strips.

PHOTO A: Attach the hang strips to the base cabinet boxes with 1½-in. drywall screws driven into the back edges of the ends and divider. Hold the hang strip top edge flush with the top edges of the cabinet ends to provide support for the seat.

PHOTO B: Build the base cabinet face frames. Lay out and cut a #20 biscuit slot at each joint. Spread glue in the joints, insert biscuits and clamp up the face frames.

❹ Build the face frames. Rip and crosscut the center and outer stiles, rails and mullions to size from birch lumber. Measure and mark the rails for the mullion joints (See the *Base Face Frames* drawing, page 90). Cut #20 biscuit slots at all the joint locations **(See Photo B)**. Apply glue to the joints, insert the biscuits, and assemble the frames with clamps.

❺ Attach the face frames to the base cabinets. Position the frame for the left cabinet so the nar-

PHOTO C: Attach the face frames to the base cabinets with glue and finish nails. Position the left cabinet frame so the narrower stile is flush with the right end of the cabinet box, leaving a ¾-in. overhang on the left end. Attach the right cabinet face frame so the center stile is flush with the left end of the cabinet and the overhang is on the right.

PHOTO D: Mill the dadoes and scribe rabbets in the upper cabinet end panels with a router and ¾-in. straight bit. Clamp one of the other end panels on top of the workpiece you are routing to serve as a straight-edge guide for the router.

rower, 1¼-in.-wide (center) stile is flush with the outer face of the the right cabinet end. The frame should overhang the left end by ¾ in. Notice in the *Left Base Face Frame/Cabinet* drawing, page 90, that the mullion should now be offset on the divider. Spread glue on the front edges of the cabinet box, clamp the face frame in place, and fasten the parts with finish nails. Position the frame for the right cabinet so the narrow center stile is flush with the left cabinet end and the ¾-in. frame overhang is on the right. Attach this face frame to the cabinet box with glue and nails **(See Photo C)**.

❻ Make and attach the finished end. Cut the end to size from birch plywood. Machine a ½-in.-deep, ¾-in.-wide rabbet along the back edge to make scribing to the wall easier. Glue and clamp the finished end in place behind the overhang on the left end of the left cabinet. Secure it with countersunk 1¼-in. screws driven from inside the cabinet.

BUILD THE UPPER CABINETS

❼ Make the ends. Cut the ends to size from birch plywood. The four end panels are machined with a pattern of dadoes and rabbets to receive the tops, bottoms, backs and recessed shelf standards (See the

Grooves in Ends drawing, page 91). The dadoes for the tops and bottoms are ⅜ in. deep, and the rabbets for the backs (and scribe) are ½ in. deep. Check your shelf standards to verify the width and depth of cut required to recess them. It's acceptable for the shelf standard dadoes to extend beyond the dadoes for the tops and bottoms, since the ends of these cuts for the standards will be hidden once the cabinets are assembled. After laying out the dadoes and rabbets, mill them in the end panels using a router and ¾-in. straight bit **(See Photo D)**.

❽ Make the remaining parts for both cabinets. Cut the tops, bottoms and backs to size. Note that the dimensions of these parts are different between the two cabinets because the left cabinet is narrower than the right.

❾ Build the cabinets. Use a hacksaw to cut the shelf standards to a length of 59¼ in., and install them in their grooves. Assemble the cabinets one at a time. Spread glue on the ends of the top and bottom for the first cabinet, position the parts in their dadoes holding the face edges flush, and clamp them in place. Secure the joints with finish nails, recessing the nail-heads with a nailset. Turn the cabinet face-side

PHOTO E: Spread glue on the front edges of the left upper cabinet box and set the face frame in place so the edges are flush with the cabinet sides. Attach the face frame with a nail gun or finish nails.

PHOTO F: Apply 1½-in.-wide strips of solid birch nosing to the front edges of the plywood shelves with glue and finish nails. Keep the top surfaces of the nosing and shelves flush.

PHOTO G: The seat is comprised of three sections of plywood joined together with #20 biscuits. Lay out and cut the biscuit joints, then glue up the long seat panel.

down, position the back in the rabbets so the top edge is flush with the cabinet top, and attach the back with glue and finish nails or countersunk 1¼-in. drywall screws. Assemble the other cabinet box using the same method.

🔟 Build the face frames. Rip and crosscut the rails and stiles to size from birch lumber. Lay out the frames so the ends of the rails fit between the stiles. Mark and cut a #20 biscuit slot at each joint. Assemble the frames with biscuits and glue, clamping the stiles and rails together with bar or pipe clamps. Check the frames for square.

⓫ Attach the face frames. Spread glue on the front edges of the cabinet boxes and clamp the frames in place (See Photo E). The left face frame will fit flush with the left cabinet sides. However, the right face frame is ¾ in. wider than the right cabinet box. Align the right face frame so the left edge is flush with the left side of the box and the overhang is on the right, to allow for wall scribing.

⓬ Make the shelves. Cut both sets of shelves to size from ¾-in. birch plywood. Rip and crosscut the nosing strips from birch lumber. Apply the nosing to the leading edges of the shelves with glue and finish nails, keeping the top edge of the nosing flush with the top face of each shelf (See Photo F).

MAKE THE SEAT PANEL

The seat is too long to be cut from one sheet of 8-ft. plywood. Although you could butt two lengths of plywood together to achieve the overall seat length, the joint will fall in the area between the two upper cabinets where it will be visible along its full length. Instead, we decided to build the seat in three sections, so the joints align with the upper cabinets and are mostly concealed by quarter-round molding.

⓭ Cut the seat sections to size, then lay out and cut #20 biscuit slots along the mating edges (See Photo G). Glue up the seat, using wide masking tape stretched across the joints or clamps linked end-to-end to hold the joints closed until the glue dries. NOTE: *Before gluing up this long panel, consider how you'll need to move it from your shop to the installation site. If its length will be a restriction, do not glue up the three panels at this stage. Assemble them on-site when you attach the seat to the base cabinet.*

⓮ Mill the seat nosing. If possible, make the front

nosing piece from a single 10-ft.-long strip of ¾ × 1½-in. birch lumber. Cut both nosing pieces generously long. Chuck a ½-in.-radius beading bit in a router table to shape the top edges of the nosing, and set the bit height to match the *Seat Nosing* profile drawing, page 90. Rout the beaded profile into both nosing strips, running them facedown through the cutter **(See Photo H)**.

PRE-FINISH THE PROJECT PARTS
We pre-finished the cabinets, seat panel, doors and nosing before installation in order to contain most of the mess to the workshop.

15 Fill recessed nail holes and any voids in the edges, surfaces or joints of the project parts. Sand, prime and paint the parts.

INSTALL THE WINDOW SEAT
16 Prepare the installation site. Carefully remove the baseboard from the area where the window seat will be installed. Pull back the carpet and pad (if any), and remove the tackless strips along the walls **(See Photo I)**.

17 Install the base cabinets. Fasten the cabinets together with 1¼-in. screws driven through the adjoining ends. If the cabinets will cover any electrical outlets, measure the locations and cut access openings in the cabinet backs. Position and level the cabinet with shims. If necessary, scribe the back edge of the finished end and the right end of the face frame in order to achieve tight joints at the walls (See page 15). Insert spacers between the hang strip and the back wall at the stud locations, and attach the cabinet to the wall with 3-in. screws driven through the hang strip into the studs **(See Photo J)**.

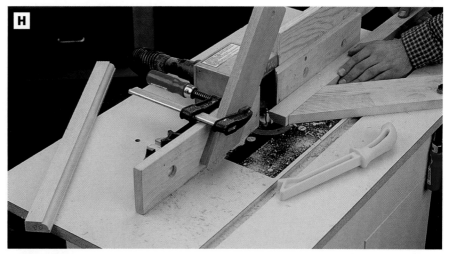

PHOTO H: Shape the top edge of the seat nosing on the router table using a ½-in.-radius beading bit. Use clamped featherboards to hold the nosing stock against the table and the fence. As you near the end of the cuts, use a pushstick to keep your fingers out of harm's way.

PHOTO I: Prepare the installation area by carefully removing the baseboard (you may want to reuse it around the project). Pull back any carpet and pad and pry up the tackless strips.

PHOTO J: Attach the base cabinets together and level the entire unit with shims. Spacers inserted between the hang strip and the back wall serve as solid installation points for fastening the cabinet to the wall. Set the shims at the wall stud locations. Fasten the base cabinets to the wall with 3-in. drywall screws driven through the hang strips and spacers.

PHOTO K: In the center portion of the window seat, drive screws into the spacers along the very back edge where they will be covered by the quarter-round molding. Secure the front edge with screws driven from inside, up through the stretchers. In the areas which will be covered by the upper cabinets, screws can be driven through the face of the seat into the cabinet ends, dividers and hang strips.

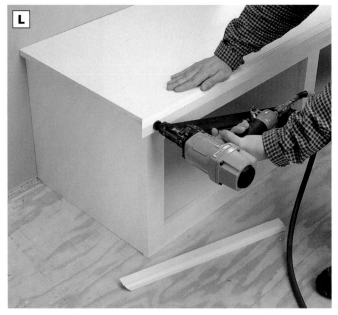

PHOTO L: Nail the seat nosing flush with the top face of the seat. The beaded edge should face up and out.

🔞 Install the seat. Set the seat panel on the base cabinets so the longest section in the glue-up is on the end that fits into the room corner. The left end of the seat should overhang the base cabinets by ½ in. Attach the seat by driving screws through the top face into the cabinet ends, dividers and hang strips or quarter round (**See Photo K**). Limit your screw locations to only those areas of the seat that will be hidden by the upper cabinets. Secure the seat beneath the front edge with 1¼-in. screws driven from inside the cabinets up through the stretchers.

🔞 Cut the seat nosing pieces to final length and miter-cut the ends that meet at the outside corner of the seat. Nail the molding to the seat with the beaded edges facing up and out. They should be flush with the seat top (**See Photo L**).

🔞 Install the upper cabinets. Position the right upper cabinet in the corner, and scribe and trim the ends and face frame stile that meet the walls, if the walls are not flat and plumb. Install the cabinet by driving 2½-in. drywall screws through the cabinet back into the wall studs (**See Photo M**). Follow the same process to install the left upper cabinet, holding the outer end 1¼ in. back from the face of the end seat nosing.

🔞 Cut and install crown molding around both upper cabinets (**See Photo N**). Cut and attach ½-in. quarter-round molding around the bases of the upper cabinets as well, to conceal the joints at the seat.

PHOTO M: Position and install the upper cabinets by driving screws through the cabinet backs into wall studs.

PHOTO N: Cut and install crown molding around the top ends of the upper cabinets as well as the top rails of the face frames. Attach the molding with a nail gun or with a hammer and nailset.

PHOTO O: After mounting the hinges on the doors, position the doors in the cabinet openings by resting the lower hinges on a ¼-in. spacer. Drill pilot holes, and fasten the hinges to the frame stiles with screws.

PHOTO P: Install new tackless strips around the perimeter of the cabinet. Leave a ⅜-in. space along the cabinet for tucking the carpet edge behind the strips.

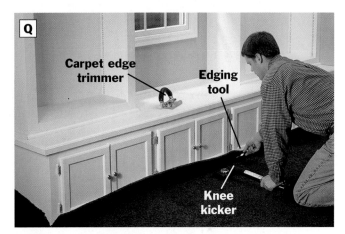

PHOTO Q: Reinstall the carpet, leaving a 4- to 6-in. overlap where it meets the cabinet. Make a relief cut at the cabinet corner so the carpet lies flat on the floor. Stretch the carpet into place with a knee kicker, press it down over the tackless strips with an edging tool, then trim it to final size with a carpet edge trimmer.

Touch up the moldings with putty, primer and paint.

㉒ Install the doors and door pulls. Lay out the hinges on the doors so they are spaced an even distance from the top and bottom door edges. To determine hinge placement, install one hinge on the face frame, holding it ¼ in. above the bottom rail. Position a door against the hinge so it overlaps both the upper and lower face frame rails by ½ in. Mark the hinge position on the door, and use this measurement as a guide for positioning and mounting all the hinges on the doors. To attach the doors to the cabinet, rest the lower hinges on a spacer cut from ¼-in. hardboard. Drill pilot holes into the edge of the stile, and fasten the hinges with screws (**See Photo O**).

㉓ Lay out and install the door knobs on the doors.

REINSTALL THE CARPET

㉔ Install new tackless strips. Nail the new tackless strips to the floor across the front and end of the cabinet, leaving a ⅜-in. space between the strips and the cabinet (**See Photo P**).

㉕ Trim the carpet to fit around the cabinet, leaving an overlap of 4 to 6 in. in both directions. Make a relief cut in the carpet at the cabinet corner so the carpet lies flat on the floor around the cabinet. Stretch the carpet into place with a knee kicker, and tuck the edges behind the tackless strip with an edging tool (**See Photo Q**). Use a carpet edge trimmer to trim away the excess for an exact fit.

㉖ Install baseboard moldings around the project to match your room moldings.

Utility Locker

Wouldn't it be great to get tools, paint and odds-and-ends off the garage floor and out of sight? This sturdy wall unit provides lots of secure, accessible storage space. It features shallow lipped shelves on both doors as well as deeper shelves in the cabinet itself. This cabinet has a place for everything, and with both doors fully opened, it's all right there at your fingertips. When not in use, your tools and hazardous materials can be securely protected behind lock and key.

Vital statistics

TYPE: Wall-mounted locker

OVERALL SIZE: 48W by 48¾H by 18D

MATERIAL: Exterior plywood

JOINERY: Butt joints reinforced with glue and screws

CONSTRUCTION DETAILS:
- Efficiently built from just three sheets of plywood
- Designed without complex joinery in order to simplify construction
- Finished inside and out to withstand damp garage or basement environments
- Fastens to wall studs with lag screws

FINISH: Exterior primer and paint

Building time

PREPARING STOCK: 0 hours

LAYOUT: 1-2 hours

CUTTING PARTS: 2-4 hours

ASSEMBLY: 3-5 hours

FINISHING: 3-5 hours

TOTAL: 9-16 hours

Shopping List

- ☐ (3) ¾ in. × 4 × 8 ft. exterior plywood
- ☐ 2 in. deck screws
- ☐ (4) 4 in. flush-mounted butt hinges
- ☐ Hasp
- ☐ (6) ¼ × 3½ in. lag screws, washers
- ☐ #10 flathead machine screws, washers, nylon lock nuts (for mounting the hinges)
- ☐ (6) ¼ × 3½ in. lag screws, washers
- ☐ Moisture-resistant wood glue
- ☐ Finishing materials

Utility Locker

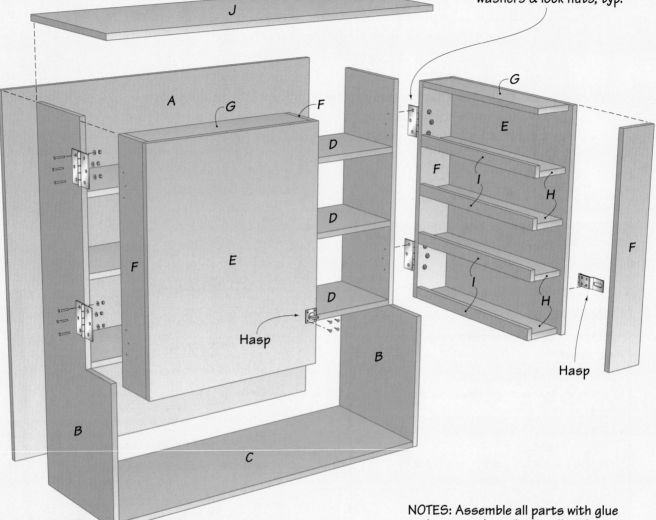

4" flush-mounted steel hinges. Attach with #10 - 24 x 1¼" machine scews, washers & lock nuts, typ.

J

A

G

F

D

G

E

F

D

F

I

H

E

D

I

H

F

Hasp

B

Hasp

B

C

NOTES: Assemble all parts with glue and screws. Attach to wall with six ¼" x 3½" lag screws & washers. Drive lag screws into wall studs.

Utility Locker Cutting List

Part	No.	Size	Material
A. Cabinet back	1	¾ × 48 × 48 in.	Exterior plywood
B. Cabinet sides	2	¾ × 16¾ × 48 in.	"
C. Cabinet bottom	1	¾ × 16¾ × 46½ in.	"
D. Cabinet shelves	3	¾ × 10⅝ × 46½ in.	"
E. Door backs	2	¾ × 23¾ × 29 in.	"
F. Door sides	4	¾ × 5¼ × 29 in.	"
G. Door tops	2	¾ × 5¼ × 22¼ in.	"
H. Door shelves	8	¾ × 4½ × 22¼ in.	"
I. Door shelf lips	8	¾ × 1½ × 22¼ in.	"
J. Cabinet top	1	¾ × 18 × 48 in.	"

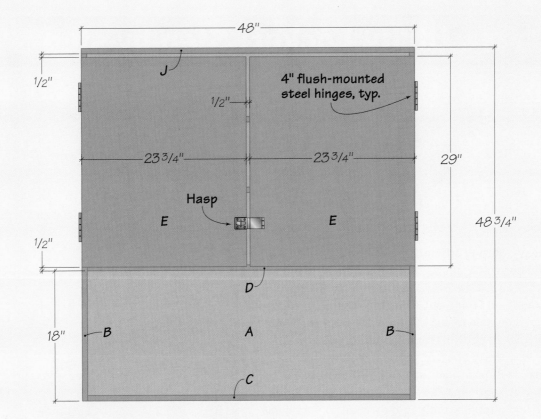

48"

1/2"

J

4" flush-mounted
steel hinges, typ.

1/2"

23³/4"   23³/4"

29"

48³/4"

Hasp

E   E

1/2"

D

18"   B   A   B

C

FRONT VIEW

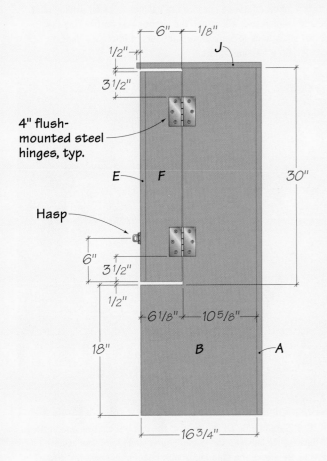

6"   1/8"

1/2"   J

3¹/2"

4" flush-
mounted steel
hinges, typ.

E   F

30"

Hasp

6"
3¹/2"
1/2"

6¹/8"   10⁵/8"

B   A

18"

16³/4"

SIDE VIEW

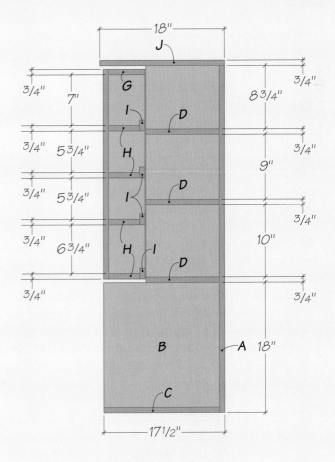

18"

J

3/4"   G   3/4"

3/4"   7"   I   D   8³/4"

3/4"   H   3/4"

3/4"   5³/4"   D   9"

3/4"   I   3/4"

3/4"   5³/4"   D

3/4"   H   I   10"

6³/4"   D

3/4"   3/4"

B   A   18"

C

17¹/2"

SIDE SECTION VIEW

Utility Locker: Step-by-step

This heavy-duty utility locker is designed to be constructed entirely from three 4 × 8 sheets of ¾-in. exterior plywood. Before actually cutting any parts, we recommend laying out a cutting scheme to ensure that you'll be able to cut all the parts from the three sheets. Also, before you begin building, think about what you want to store in your cabinet; we have specified shelf positions that make efficient use of the interior space and facilitate storing many kinds of tools and supplies, but you may want to vary some of the shelf positions depending on your specific storage needs.

This project consists of three structures—the basic cabinet and two doors—which are built individually and then joined to form the completed cabinet.

BUILD THE CABINET

❶ Lay out and cut out the cabinet parts—the back, sides, bottom, shelves and top. The safest way to cut down full-size plywood sheets is to use a circular saw guided along a clamped straightedge. When cutting the side pieces to their final "L" shape, make the primary cuts with a circular saw and finish the inside corners with a handsaw or jig saw.

❷ On the cabinet sides, mark centerlines for drilling pilot holes for the screws that will attach the bottom and the shelves. Place the sides back-to-back on your worksurface with their ends aligned, measure and mark the screw hole locations, and use a framing square as a guide to extend reference lines across both plywood pieces at one time (**See Photo A**). See the *Side Section View* drawing, page 101, for locating the cabinet shelf positions.

❸ Begin assembling the cabinet. Stand the side pieces on their back edges on your worksurface so your screw layout lines face outward. Spread an even layer of glue on the ends of the shelves and bottom.

PHOTO A: Mark reference lines on the cabinet sides for drilling pilot holes for screws that will attach the shelves and bottom. Lay the cabinet sides back-to-back. Draw both sets of reference lines at once with a framing square.

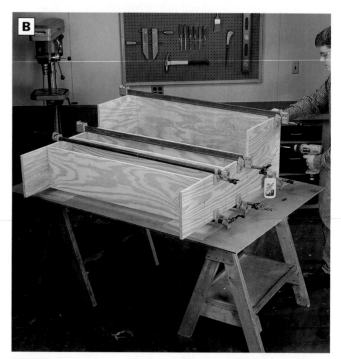

PHOTO B: Spread glue on the ends of the cabinet shelves and bottom, set these parts between the cabinet sides and clamp the assembly together. Reinforce the glue joints with countersunk screws, driven through the cabinet sides.

PHOTO C: Lay the cabinet facedown on a pair of sawhorses or another suitable worksurface. Spread glue along the back edges of the shelves and bottom. Clamp the back in place and drive countersunk screws through the back into the shelves and bottom.

PHOTO D: Glue a strip of shelf nosing along one long edge of each 8-ft. piece of shelving to form a long shelf blank. Clamp the nosing in place so one edge is flush with one of the shelf faces.

Clamp the shelves and bottom into position between the sides. Drill countersunk pilot holes along your reference lines, and fasten the pieces together with 2-in. deck screws (**See Photo B**). Remove the clamps.

❹ Attach the cabinet back. Turn the cabinet over and apply glue to the back edges of the bottom, shelves and sides. Clamp the back in place, using it to square up the cabinet box. Draw reference lines across the back to mark the shelf positions for locating screws. Fasten the back to the cabinet with screws driven into countersunk pilot holes (**See Photo C**). Use plenty of screws when fastening the back to the sides, shelves and bottom—all the weight of the cabinet and its contents will be supported by the back when the cabinet hangs on the wall.

❺ Install the cabinet top. Stand the cabinet right-side-up on the floor, apply glue to the top edges of the sides and back, then position the top so its back edge and ends are flush. Drill countersunk pilot holes and attach the top to the cabinet with screws.

BUILD THE DOORS
The doors are actually two small shelf units. The door shelves are lipped along the front edges to prevent items from sliding off when the doors swing.

❻ Make the door shelf stock. Rip two pieces of ply-

wood 4½ in. wide × 96 in. long for the shelves. Rip two additional pieces 1½ in. wide × 96 in. long for the shelf nosing. Glue a nosing strip to the edge of each shelf strip, holding the pieces in place with clamps until the glue dries (**See Photo D**).

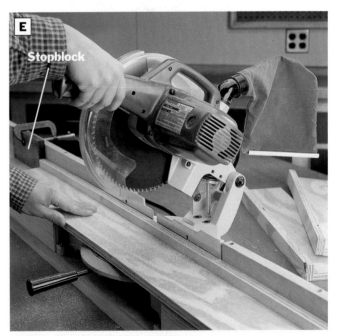

PHOTO E: Cut the door shelves to length. We used a power miter saw with a stopblock clamped to the fence so the shelf lengths would match. Incidentally, you can use the same stopblock setting for cutting the door tops to length.

PHOTO F: Glue and clamp the door sides, top and shelves together, then drive countersunk 2-in. screws through the door sides to reinforce all the door joints. Once the door frames are assembled, attach the door backs to the frames with glue and screws.

PHOTO G: Conceal all screwheads with wood filler, sand the entire cabinet and apply a coat of primer followed by two coats of paint. If moisture resistance or appearance aren't concerns for you, you could also leave the cabinet unfinished.

7 Cut the door shelves to length. Clamp a stopblock to the fence of a power miter saw to ensure that all the shelves will be exactly the same length (**See Photo E**). You could also cut the shelves with a circular saw or a table saw. However you make these cuts, be sure the shelf lengths are equal.

8 Cut the remaining door parts— the backs, sides and tops—to size.

9 On the door sides, mark screw-hole centerlines for attaching the shelves and the tops. Assuming the shelf positions are identical for both door units, the door sides can be quickly and accurately gang-marked by laying the parts side by side with their ends aligned.

10 Assemble the door parts. Spread glue on the ends of the shelves and top, and clamp them in place between the pairs of sides. Drill countersunk pilot holes along the centerlines, and fasten the parts together with deck screws (**See Photo F**).

11 Attach the door backs. Measure and mark screw hole centerlines on the door backs. Apply glue to the back edges of the sides, shelves and top. Set the door backs into place, using them to square up the door frames. Drill countersunk pilot holes and attach the backs to the door frames with screws.

FINISH THE CABINET & DOORS

12 Fill the screw holes and any voids in the plywood edges with wood filler. Once the filler dries, sand all surfaces and edges. Apply primer and two coats of exterior paint (**See Photo G**).

MOUNT THE DOORS

Since the doors are heavy, the hinges attach to the doors and cabinet with #10 machine screws, washers and nylon lock nuts.

⓭ Install the doors. Lay the cabinet on its back and use ⅛-in.-thick shims for spacing the doors out from the cabinet. Position the doors top-to-bottom and left-to-right. Use the *Side View* drawing, page 101, for locating the four corner holes of each hinge on the cabinet. Fasten the hinges temporarily with wood screws. Drill the remaining hinge holes to accept the machine screws, and install the screws with washers and lock nuts **(See Photo H)**. Remove the wood screws and replace them with machine screws, washers and nylon lock nuts.

⓮ Position and attach the hasp to the door backs using the screws provided with the hasp.

INSTALL THE CABINET

When positioning the cabinet on the garage wall, consider three factors: A) The height of the cabinet off the floor—is there enough space for whatever you want to store below it? B) The overall width of the cabinet with the doors open—is there enough room for full access to the cabinet? C) Sufficient support; try to position the cabinet so you can fasten it to three studs if possible, and definitely to no fewer than two.

⓯ Prop the cabinet securely in place against the wall and level it. Drill ¼-in. pilot holes through the cabinet back into the wall studs, and attach the cabinet to the wall with 3½-in. lag screws and washers **(See Photo I)**.

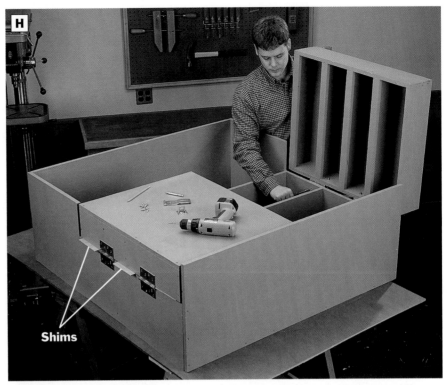

PHOTO H: Mount the doors to the cabinet. Set ⅛-in.-thick shims between the doors and the cabinet first, locate the hinge positions and attach the hinges temporarily with a few wood screws. Drill pilot holes for machine screws that will attach the hinges to the cabinet parts. Then install the machine screws with washers and nylon lock nuts to ensure strong connections.

PHOTO I: Select a spot for the cabinet that allows you to open the doors fully while providing at least two wall studs for mounting purposes. Position and level the cabinet on the wall. Then drive ¼ × 3½-in. lag screws through the cabinet back and into the wall studs.

Room Divider

Many otherwise wonderful homes suffer from having the main door open directly into the living space, making it difficult to keep entryway clutter in its place. Here's a project that solves that problem and actually remodels your home. While it serves a host of specific practical functions with its seat, mirror, bookshelves and top display shelf, it also divides your living room from your entry, improving the appearance and utility of both.

Vital statistics

TYPE: Room divider

OVERALL SIZE: 63L by 78H by 28D

MATERIAL: Red oak, red oak plywood, fir plywood, 2 × 4's, oak molding, mirror

JOINERY: Butt joints reinforced with glue and screws or dowels

CONSTRUCTION DETAILS:
- Frame-and-panel construction featuring dowel joints
- Panels sandwich between cleats fastened to the face frames and stop molding
- Panels fasten in place after the bookcase and bench assemblies are installed
- Rabbets on bookshelf and bench stiles allow for scribing and trimming for a flush fit to wall
- Solid-wood seat fastens to bench with seat cleats to allow for seasonal wood movement
- Project fastens to floor and wall with concealed 2 × 4 installation cleats
- Match project base molding to your room's existing base molding

FINISH: Stain and polyurethane to match surrounding woodwork

Building time

PREPARING STOCK: 4-6 hours

LAYOUT: 6-8 hours

CUTTING PARTS: 11-14 hours

ASSEMBLY: 11-13 hours

FINISHING: 10-12 hours

INSTALLATION: 8-10 hours

TOTAL: 50-63 hours

Shopping List

- [ ] (1) ¾ in. × 4 × 4 ft. fir plywood
- [ ] (3) 2 × 4 in. × 8 ft. dimension lumber
- [ ] (2) ¾ in. × 4 × 8 ft. red oak plywood
- [ ] (1) ¼ in. × 4 × 8 ft. red oak plywood
- [ ] (8) ¾ × 6 in. × 8 ft. red oak
- [ ] (5) ¾ × 4 in. × 8 ft. red oak
- [ ] 15 bd. ft. ¾ in. red oak (for seat)
- [ ] (2) ⁹⁄₁₆ × 2 in. × 8 ft. oak cove molding
- [ ] (7) ⅜ × ⅜ in. × 8 ft. oak quarter round
- [ ] (1) ¾ × ¾ in. × 8 ft. oak quarter round
- [ ] (2) ⅝ × 1⁹⁄₁₆ in. × 8 ft. oak panel mold
- [ ] (1) ¼ × 30 × 36 in. mirror
- [ ] (16) Brass shelf pins
- [ ] ⅜-in.-dia. × 1½-in. dowel pins
- [ ] Drywall screws (3-, 1¾-, 1⅝-, 1¼-in.)
- [ ] #10 × 1¼-in. panhead screws, washers
- [ ] Wall anchors
- [ ] #10 biscuits
- [ ] Wood glue
- [ ] Finishing materials

Room Divider

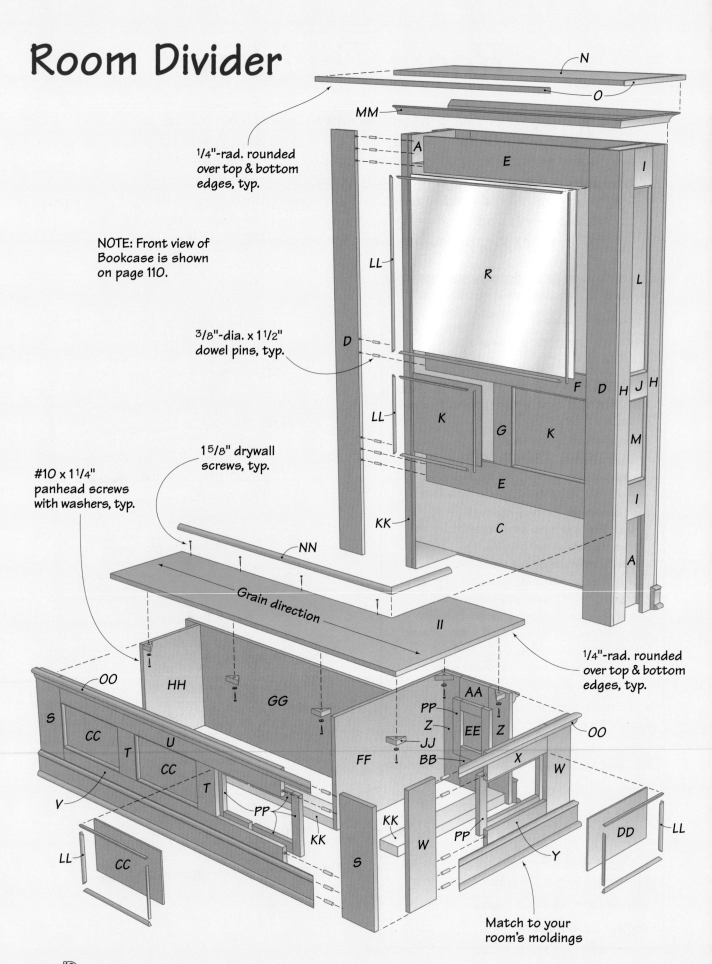

N

O

MM

A

E

I

1/4"-rad. rounded over top & bottom edges, typ.

LL

R

NOTE: Front view of Bookcase is shown on page 110.

L

D

3/8"-dia. x 1 1/2" dowel pins, typ.

LL

F

D

H

J

H

K

G

K

M

1 5/8" drywall screws, typ.

E

I

KK

C

A

#10 x 1 1/4" panhead screws with washers, typ.

NN

Grain direction

II

1/4"-rad. rounded over top & bottom edges, typ.

OO

HH

GG

AA

OO

PP

S

Z

EE

Z

CC

T

U

JJ

X

W

CC

FF

BB

T

V

PP

KK

KK

W

PP

Y

DD

LL

LL

CC

S

Match to your room's moldings

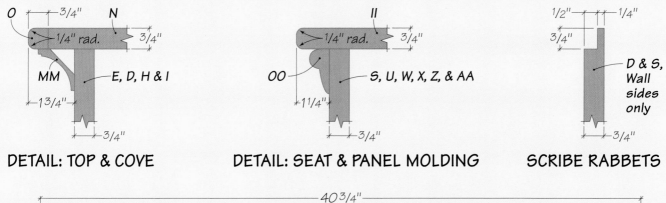

DETAIL: TOP & COVE   DETAIL: SEAT & PANEL MOLDING   SCRIBE RABBETS

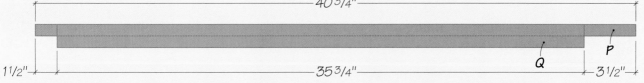

DETAIL: SHELF & NOSING ALIGNMENT

Room Divider Cutting List

Part	No.	Size	Material
BOOKCASE			
A. Sides	2	¾ × 11½ × 77¼ in.	Oak plywood
B. Top/bottom	2	¾ × 11¼ × 41 in.	"
C. Back	1	¼ × 41 × 67¼ in.	"
D. Front/back stiles	4	¾ × 6 × 77¼ in.	Oak
E. Front/back wide rails	4	¾ × 6 × 36 in.	"
F. Back center rail	1	¾ × 4 × 36 in.	"
G. Mullion	1	¾ × 4 × 14 in.	"
H. End stiles	2	¾ × 3¼ × 77¼ in.	"
I. End wide rails	2	¾ × 6 × 5 in.	"
J. End center rail	1	¾ × 4 × 5 in.	"
K. Back panels	2	¼ × 16 × 14 in.	Oak plywood
L. Upper end panel	1	¼ × 5 × 30 in.	"
M. Lower end panel	1	¼ × 5 × 14 in.	"
N. Top	1	¾ × 15 × 49 in.	"
O. Top nosing		¾ × ¾ × 10 lin. ft.	Oak
P. Shelves	4	¾ × 11¼ × 40¾ in.	Oak plywood
Q. Shelf nosing	4	¾ × 1½ × 35¾ in.	Oak
R. Mirror	1	¼ × 30 × 36 in.	
BENCH			
S. Long panel end stiles	2	¾ × 6 × 17¼ in.	Oak
T. Mullions	2	¾ × 4 × 7¼ in.	"
U. Long panel top rail	1	¾ × 4 × 49¾ in.	"
V. Long panel lower rail	1	¾ × 6 × 49¾ in.	"
W. End panel stiles	2	¾ × 5¼ × 17¼ in.	Oak

Part	No.	Size	Material
X. End panel top rail	1	¾ × 4 × 13 in.	Oak
Y. End panel lower rail	1	¾ × 6 × 13 in.	"
Z. Short panel stiles	2	¾ × 4 × 17¼ in.	"
AA. Short panel top rail	1	¾ × 4 × 5¾ in.	"
BB. Short panel lower rail	1	¾ × 6 × 5¾ in.	"
CC. Long panels	3	¼ × 13⅞ × 7¼ in.	Oak plywood
DD. End panel	1	¼ × 13 × 7¼ in.	"
EE. Short panel	1	¼ × 5¾ × 7¼ in.	"
FF. Divider	1	¾ × 17¼ × 23½ in.	Fir plywood
GG. Back	1	¾ × 17¼ × 47 in.	"
HH. Internal end	1	¾ × 17¼ × 12¼ in.	"
II. Seat	1	¾ × 27½ × 63 in.	Oak
JJ. Seat cleats	6	¾ × 2 × 2 in.	"
OTHER CLEATS, STOPS, MOLDINGS			
KK. Installation cleats		1½ × 3½ × 24 lin. ft.	Fir 2 × 4's
LL. Panel/mirror stop		⅜ × ⅜ × 52 lin. ft.	Oak quarter round
MM. Cove molding		9/16 × 2 × 10 lin. ft.	Oak
NN. Over-seat molding		¾ × ¾ × 5 lin. ft.	Oak quarter round
OO. Under-seat molding		⅝ × 1 9/16 × 10 lin. ft.	Oak panel mold
PP. Panel backer cleats		¾ × 1½ × various	Scrap

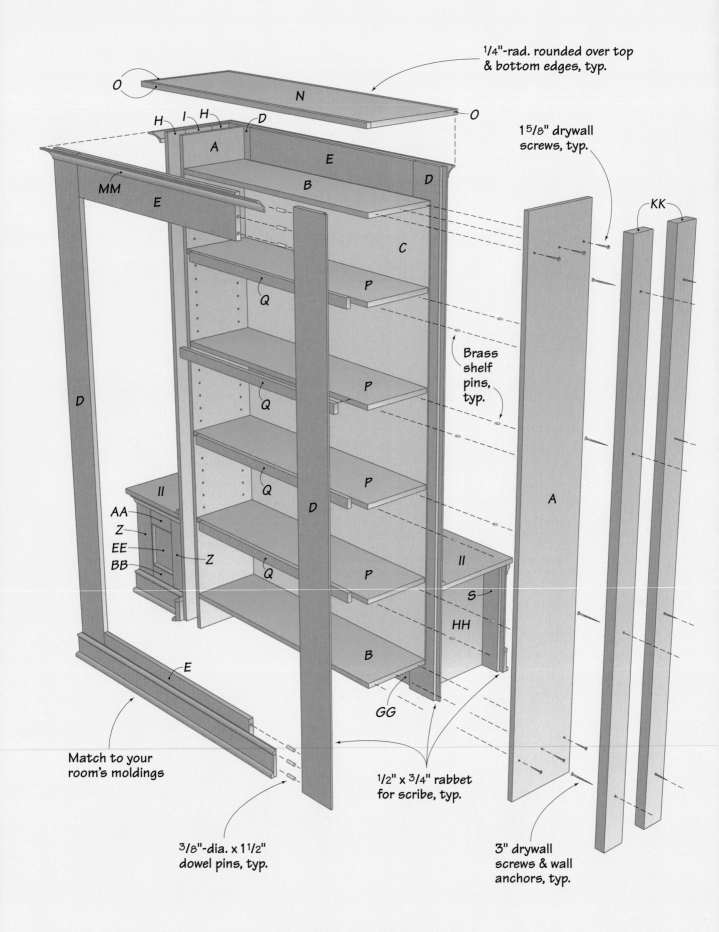

¼"-rad. rounded over top
& bottom edges, typ.

O

H I H   D

A

E

B

D

MM

E

1⅝" drywall
screws, typ.

KK

C

Q

P

Brass
shelf
pins,
typ.

D

Q

P

Q

P

A

II

AA

Z

EE

BB   Z

Q   D

P

II

S

HH

E

B

GG

Match to your
room's moldings

O

N

O

½" x ¾" rabbet
for scribe, typ.

3" drywall
screws & wall
anchors, typ.

⅜"-dia. x 1½"
dowel pins, typ.

BOOKCASE FRONT VIEW

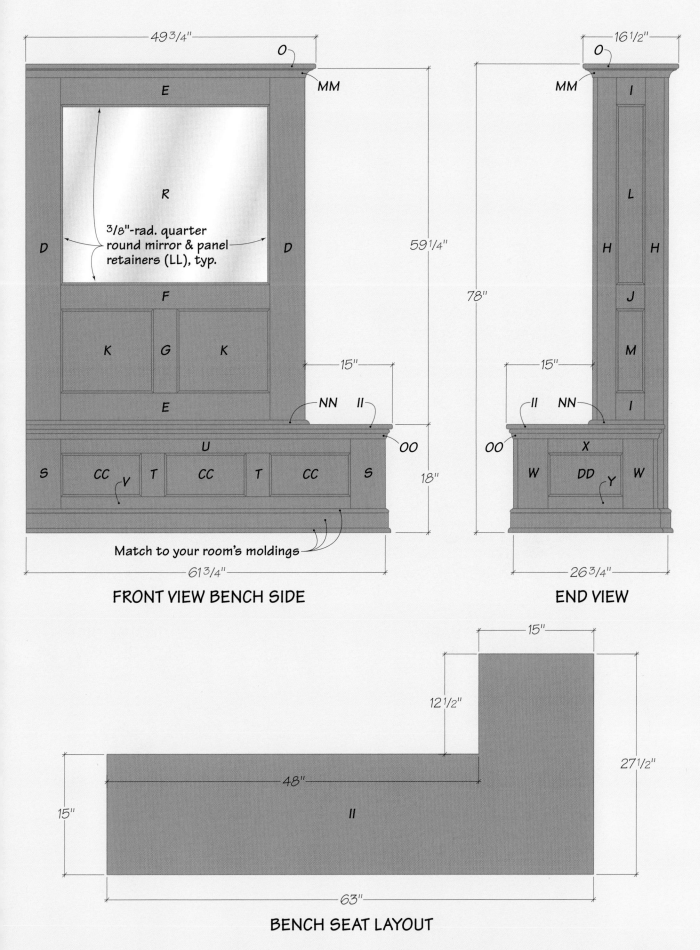

49 3/4"

O

MM

E

R

3/8"-rad. quarter
round mirror & panel
retainers (LL), typ.

D   D

F

K   G   K

E

59 1/4"

15"

NN   II

OO

U

S   CC   T   CC   T   CC   S

V

18"

Match to your room's moldings

61 3/4"

FRONT VIEW BENCH SIDE

16 1/2"

O

MM

I

L

H   H

J

M

15"

II   NN

I

OO

X

W   DD   W

Y

78"

26 3/4"

END VIEW

15"

12 1/2"

48"

II

27 1/2"

15"

63"

BENCH SEAT LAYOUT

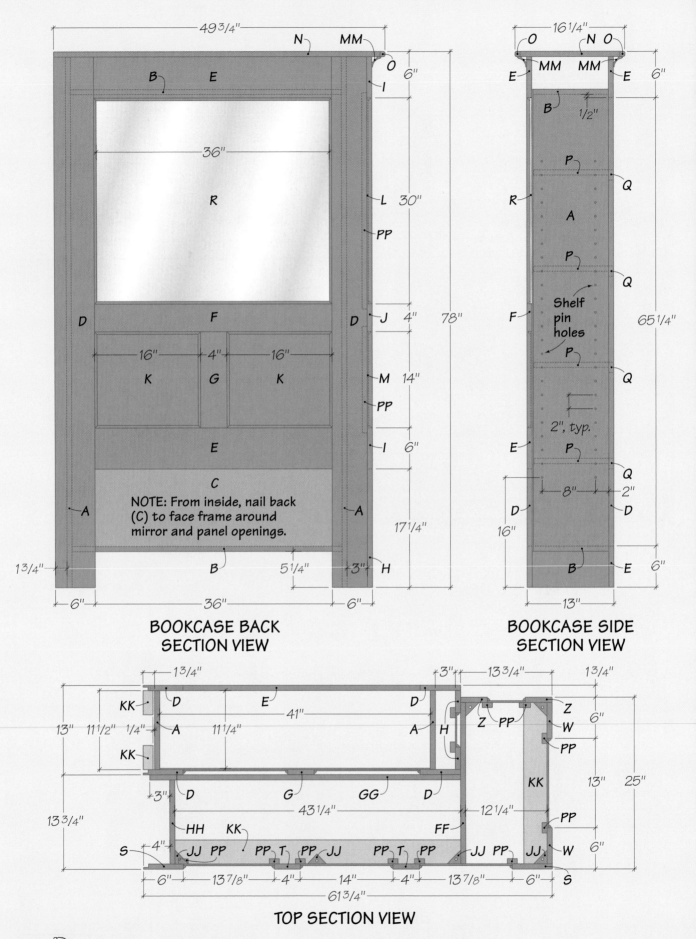

BOOKCASE BACK SECTION VIEW

49³/₄"

N

MM

B

E

O

I

6"

36"

R

L   30"

PP

78"

D

F

D

J   4"

16"   4"   16"

K   G   K

M   14"

PP

E

I   6"

C

NOTE: From inside, nail back (C) to face frame around mirror and panel openings.

A

A

B

1³/₄"

5¹/₄"

3"   H

17¹/₄"

6"   36"   6"

BOOKCASE SIDE SECTION VIEW

16¹/₄"

O

N   O

E   MM   MM   E

6"

B

¹/₂"

P

Q

R

A

P

Q

F   Shelf pin holes

P

Q

65¹/₄"

2", typ.

E

P

Q

8"   2"

D   D

16"

B   E   6"

13"

TOP SECTION VIEW

1³/₄"

3"   13³/₄"   1³/₄"

KK   D   E   D   Z

13"   Z   PP   6"

11¹/₂"   ¹/₄"   A   11¹/₄"   41"   A   H   W

KK   PP

3"   D   G   GG   D   KK   13"   25"

43¹/₄"   12¹/₄"

13³/₄"   HH   KK   PP

S   4"   JJ   PP   PP   T   PP   JJ   PP   T   PP   JJ   PP   JJ   W

6"   13⁷/₈"   4"   14"   4"   13⁷/₈"   6"   S

FF   6"

61³/₄"

so the seat will fit flush to the wall. Fasten the seat in place with 1¼-in. panhead wood screws and washers driven from inside the bench through the seat cleats (**See Photo J**).

22 Make the top. The top consists of a center plywood panel wrapped on both long edges and one end with ¾ × ¾-in. oak nosing to conceal the plywood edges. Cut the plywood panel to size and rip and crosscut the three strips of oak nosing. Miter-cut the ends of the nosing pieces at 45° to fit around the plywood top. Attach the nosing to the top with #10 biscuits and glue. Clamp the nosing in place (**See Photo K**). Rout a ¼-in. roundover on the top and bottom edges of the nosing. Sand and finish the top.

23 Set the top in place over the bookcase to allow for an even overhang, and fasten the top to the bookcase with countersunk 1¼-in. drywall screws.

24 Miter-cut three lengths of cove molding to fit around the joint between the top and bookcase. Stain and varnish these molding pieces, and fasten them in place with finish nails.

ADD THE MIRROR, PANELS & MOLDINGS

25 Cut strips of over-seat and under-seat molding to length, miter-cut the ends where they meet in the corners, test their fit, then apply finish. Attach the molding with brads and a nail gun or finish nails.

26 Install the mirror. Miter-cut four pieces of panel/stop molding to size, apply finish and secure the mirror in place with the stop moldings and brads or finish nails.

27 Cut, fit, finish and install baseboard around the bench to match your surrounding woodwork.

28 Cut the five bench panels and four bookcase panels to size from ¼-in. plywood, and test their fit in the panel openings.

29 Miter-cut four strips of panel/mirror stop for each panel, to hold the panels in place. Then sand and finish the panels and stop moldings.

30 Install the panels. Attach the panel stop with brads and a nail gun or finish nails (**See Photo L**).

31 Install the shelf clips and the adjustable shelves.

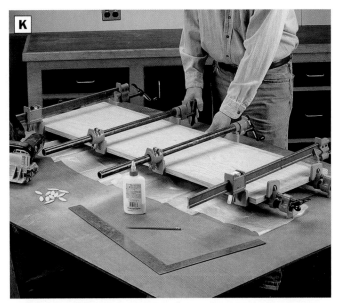

PHOTO K: Cut #10 biscuit slots in the oak nosing and plywood top, spread glue along the mating surfaces of the parts and clamp the assembly together with biscuits inserted in the slots.

PHOTO L: Install the mirror and oak panels into their openings with ⅜ × ⅜-in. panel/stop molding and brads or finish nails.

Custom Closet

Good storage space will no longer be scarce when you build this generous closet with its wide sliding doors. Stored items are readily accessible, even in tight quarters. Designed to be installed either in the corner of a room or on an open wall with both ends exposed, this closet has shelves that are sturdy enough to comfortably handle your heaviest items. This project is budget-friendly too—the slab-style doors are pre-fabricated hollow-core and the walls are made of inexpensive lauan plywood.

Vital statistics

TYPE: Built-in closet

OVERALL SIZE: 99½W by 83¾H by 27¾D

MATERIAL: Plywood, pine, hollow-core doors

JOINERY: Butt joints reinforced with glue and screws

CONSTRUCTION DETAILS:
· Dimensions of upright components can be modified to suit either a 7- or 8-ft. ceiling
· Plywood shelves are reinforced with struts and spreaders
· Pre-fabricated hollow-core doors eliminate the need for building these parts
· Doors are hung on sliding-door hardware

FINISH: Paint, stain, polyurethane varnish

Building time

PREPARING STOCK: 0 hours

LAYOUT: 1-2 hours

CUTTING PARTS: 1-2 hours

ASSEMBLY: 4-6 hours

FINISHING: 2-4 hours

TOTAL: 8-14 hours

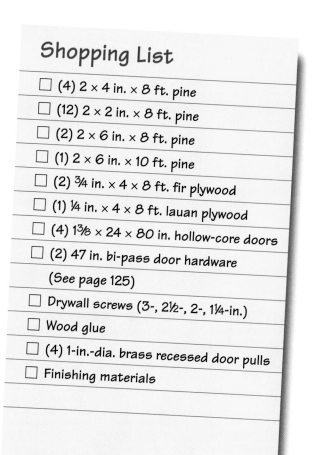

Shopping List

- ☐ (4) 2 × 4 in. × 8 ft. pine
- ☐ (12) 2 × 2 in. × 8 ft. pine
- ☐ (2) 2 × 6 in. × 8 ft. pine
- ☐ (1) 2 × 6 in. × 10 ft. pine
- ☐ (2) ¾ in. × 4 × 8 ft. fir plywood
- ☐ (1) ¼ in. × 4 × 8 ft. lauan plywood
- ☐ (4) 1⅜ × 24 × 80 in. hollow-core doors
- ☐ (2) 47 in. bi-pass door hardware (See page 125)
- ☐ Drywall screws (3-, 2½-, 2-, 1¼-in.)
- ☐ Wood glue
- ☐ (4) 1-in.-dia. brass recessed door pulls
- ☐ Finishing materials

Custom
Closet

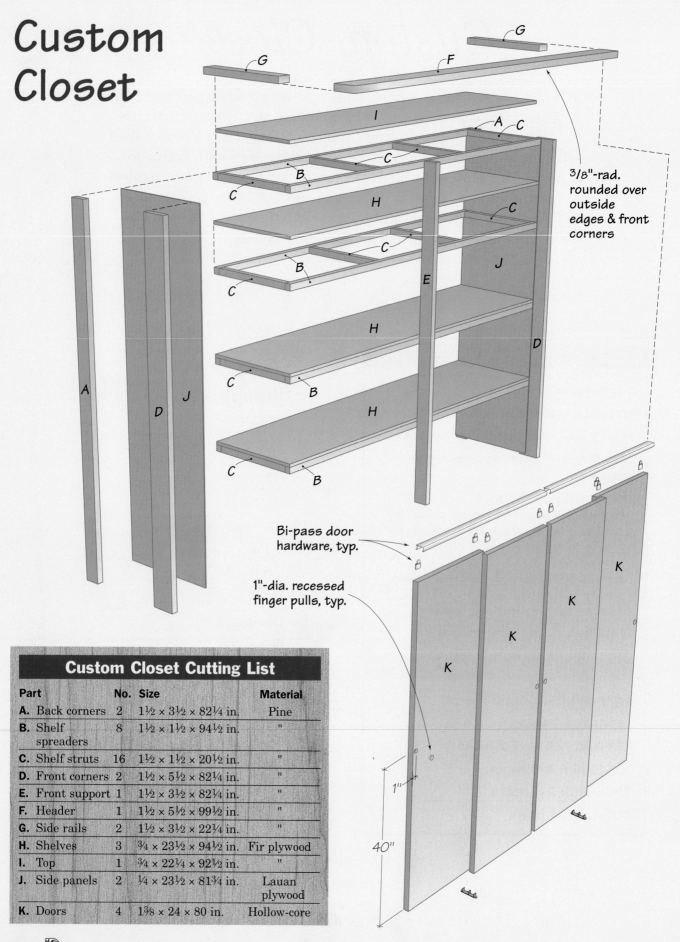

3/8"-rad. rounded over outside edges & front corners

Bi-pass door hardware, typ.

1"-dia. recessed finger pulls, typ.

1"

40"

Custom Closet Cutting List

Part	No.	Size	Material
A. Back corners	2	1½ × 3½ × 82¼ in.	Pine
B. Shelf spreaders	8	1½ × 1½ × 94½ in.	"
C. Shelf struts	16	1½ × 1½ × 20½ in.	"
D. Front corners	2	1½ × 5½ × 82¼ in.	"
E. Front support	1	1½ × 3½ × 82¼ in.	"
F. Header	1	1½ × 5½ × 99½ in.	"
G. Side rails	2	1½ × 3½ × 22¼ in.	"
H. Shelves	3	¾ × 23½ × 94½ in.	Fir plywood
I. Top	1	¾ × 22¼ × 92½ in.	"
J. Side panels	2	¼ × 23½ × 81¾ in.	Lauan plywood
K. Doors	4	1⅜ × 24 × 80 in.	Hollow-core

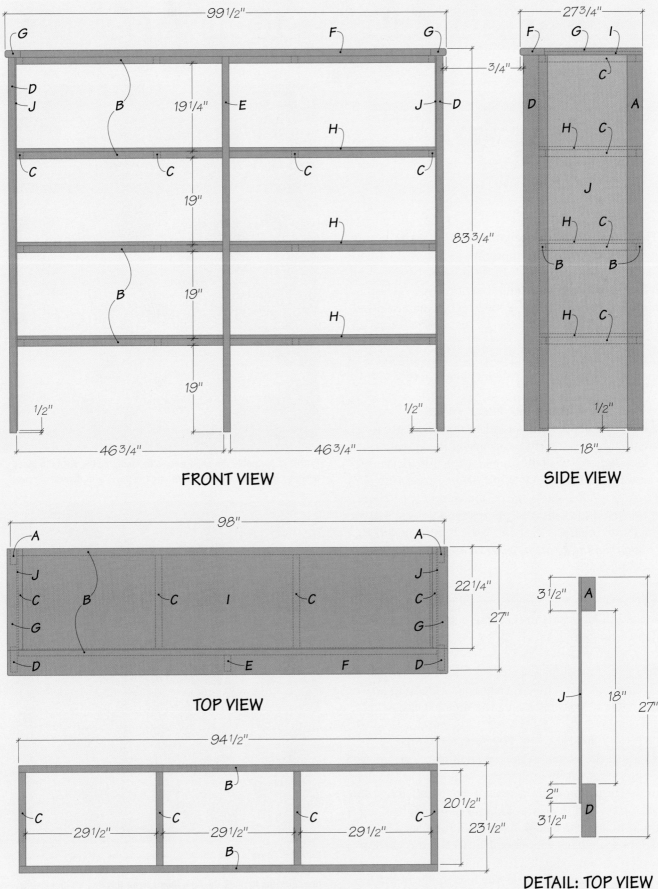

99 1/2"

G

F

G

3/4"

D

J

B

19 1/4"

E

H

J

D

C

C

C

C

H

19"

B

19"

H

19"

1/2"

46 3/4"

46 3/4"

1/2"

83 3/4"

FRONT VIEW

27 3/4"

F

G

I

C

D

A

H

C

J

H

C

B

B

H

C

1/2"

18"

SIDE VIEW

98"

A

A

J

J

C

B

C

I

C

C

G

G

D

E

F

D

22 1/4"

27"

TOP VIEW

94 1/2"

B

C

C

C

C

29 1/2"

29 1/2"

29 1/2"

B

20 1/2"

23 1/2"

DETAIL: SHELF SUPPORT FRAMES

3 1/2"

A

J

18"

27"

2"

D

3 1/2"

**DETAIL: TOP VIEW
OF CLOSET SIDES**

Custom Closet: Step-by-step

This closet project is designed so it can be built and installed virtually anywhere. We built ours in a basement, but it also could be built in a bedroom or, with minor modifications, even in an entryway. We installed our closet in a corner, but the plan is developed so the closet could also be installed with both ends exposed. For a more formal appearance, you could use oak veneer end panels or louvered doors instead of the lauan slab doors shown here.

MAKE THE SHELF PARTS

1 Cut the eight shelf spreaders and 16 struts to length. Mark the strut positions on the spreaders, and assemble the shelf frames using 3-in. drywall screws **(See Photo A)**. NOTE: *Before proceeding with this step, double-check the dimensions of your 2 × 2s. If the actual dimensions are less than 1½ × 1½ in. (we have seen them as scant as 1⅜ × 1⅜ in.) you will need to lengthen the struts in order to keep the specified shelf depth.*

2 Cut the shelves and top to size from ¾-in. plywood. Fill any voids in the front edges, and sand the panels smooth.

3 Prime and paint the shelves and shelf frames. We recommend using a light color so stored items will be as visible as possible inside the finished closet.

INSTALL THE TOP SHELF FRAME

4 Mark the height of the top shelf frame on the wall. To do this, start by finding the high point of the floor in the area where the closet will be installed by comparing several floor-to-ceiling measurements along the wall. Measure 80¾ in. up from the floor's high point on the back wall **(See Photo B)**, and mark a level line that extends 99 in. from the room corner. (This reference line marks the lower edge of the top shelf frame.) Mark the wall stud locations along the

PHOTO A: Assemble the shelf frames by clamping the struts in place between the spreaders and fastening the parts with drywall screws.

PHOTO B: Make a level reference line along the back wall to establish the location of the top shelf. Measure up from the high point of the floor 80¾ in. to mark the line. Then extend this line 99 in. out from the corner.

reference line so you'll know where to drive screws to fasten the top shelf frame.

❺ Install the top shelf frame. Position the frame on the wall, 2½ in. out from the corner, keeping the lower edge of the back spreader even with your reference line. Install the frame by driving 3-in. drywall screws into the wall studs (See Photo C). Clamp temporary 2 × 4 supports to the front edge of the frame to hold it in place.

❻ Adjust the shelf frame so it is level front-to-back and side-to-side. Measure down from the front corners (See Photo D) to confirm the actual length of the front corner pieces (length may vary slightly from the specified length on the *Cutting List,* page 120, if your floor is uneven or out of level). Adjusting the length of these pieces now will allow you to install them without shims.

BUILD & INSTALL THE SIDE PANELS

❼ Cut the front and back corner pieces and front support to length. Finish these parts with primer and paint. If you're installing the closet on a damp basement floor, paint the bottom ends of these pieces to limit the amount of moisture they absorb.

❽ Cut the side panel pieces to size and apply the finish of your choice at this time. Since the doors will receive the same topcoat treatment, finish them at this time as well.

❾ Assemble the side panels. Align the back corner pieces flush with the back edges of the side panels. Arrange the front corner pieces so they extend 3½ in. beyond the front edges of the side panels. Keep the top edge of the panels even with the top ends of the corner pieces. NOTE: *The side panels are ½ in. shorter than the corner pieces so the bottom edge of the side panels will align with the bottoms of the doors when installation is complete.* Fasten each panel to the corner pieces with 1¼-in. screws driven through the panel into the corner pieces (See Photo E).

❿ Measure and mark the shelf frame locations on the inside faces of both side panels. Take your measurements down from the top end of the panels.

⓫ Attach the side panels to the top shelf frame with 3-in. drywall screws driven from inside the shelf struts into the corner pieces. Keep the top of the side panels flush with the top of the shelf frame.

PHOTO C: With assistance, attach the top shelf frame to the wall. Hold it 2½ in. out from the room corner, align the lower edge with your level reference line, drill countersunk pilot holes and fasten with 3-in. drywall screws driven into the wall studs.

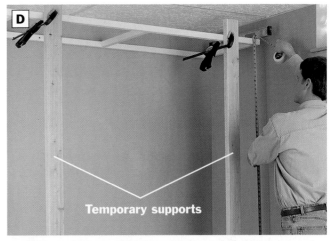

PHOTO D: Use temporary supports clamped to the shelf frame to help level it. Then measure from the floor to the top four corners of the frame to confirm the length of the front and back corner pieces.

PHOTO E: Attach the side panels to the front and back corner pieces with screws. The top ends of the parts should be flush, and the front corner pieces should overhang the side panels by 3½ in. (See the *Detail: Top View of Closet Sides* drawing, page 121).

PHOTO F: Attach the bottom shelf frame to the side panels, using your reference lines on the sides for aligning the parts. Then measure down the wall from the top frame to verify that the bottom frame does not sag or bow before attaching it to the wall studs.

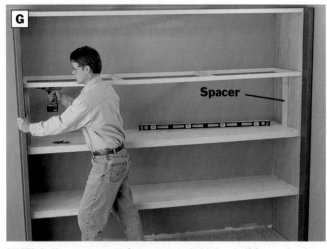

PHOTO G: Use spacers cut from scrap to hold the shelf frames in place while you fasten them to the side panels. Check for level before attaching each one.

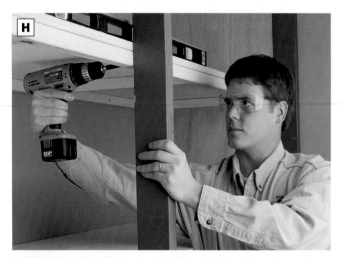

PHOTO H: Install the front support by first clamping it in place against the shelves and then driving screws from inside the closet through the shelf spreaders.

INSTALL THE REMAINING SHELVES

12 Line up the bottom shelf frame with your reference lines on the side panels and screw it in place. Measure down the wall from the top frame to double-check the location of the bottom shelf frame on the wall **(See Photo F)**. If the bottom frame is bowing or sagging along its length, adjust the back shelf spreader up or down on the wall, hold it in place and fasten it to the wall studs with screws.

13 Position the bottom shelf on the frame and attach from underneath the frame with 2-in. drywall screws.

14 Position and attach the remaining frames and shelves. To make this process easy, work up from the bottom shelf using spacers cut from scrap to prop each frame in position. Attach the frames to the side panels **(See Photo G)** and back wall, then fasten the shelves to the frames.

15 Install the front support. Mark its location on the front edges of the shelf frames, checking to ensure that it is plumb so the doors will close evenly against it. Attach the support by driving 3-in. screws from the back through the frames **(See Photo H)**.

MAKE & ATTACH THE HEADER

16 Cut the header and side rails to length. Round over the top and bottom outside edges of the header and side rails with a router and piloted ⅜-in. roundover bit. **(See Photo I)**. Sand these parts smooth, and finish them with primer and paint.

17 Install the side rails. Each rail should overhang the closet sides by ¾ in. and butt up against the back wall. Fasten the rails by driving 2½-in. screws up through the end shelf struts and into the rails.

18 Install the header and top panel. Clamp the header in place against the side rails, so the front edge evenly overhangs the corner pieces and the front support. Attach the header by driving screws up through the front shelf spreader **(See Photo J)**. Set the top panel into place and fasten it with 2-in. drywall screws driven up through the shelf struts. The top can also rest in place without screws.

INSTALL THE SLIDING DOORS

19 Install the bi-pass door tracks, following the manufacturer's instructions (See next page). If necessary, trim the metal tracks to length with a hacksaw so they fit in between the front corner pieces and the

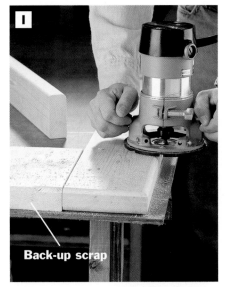

PHOTO I: Round-over the outside top and bottom edges of the header and side rails with a router and piloted roundover bit. To minimize tearout and control the length of cut, clamp a scrap against each workpiece where the roundover should end before you rout it.

PHOTO J: With the side rails installed and the header clamped in place, fasten the header by driving screws up through the top shelf spreader. Then remove the clamps and drop the top panel into place.

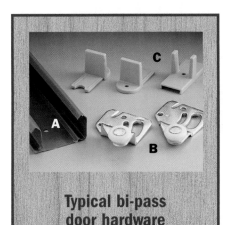

Typical bi-pass door hardware

Inexpensive bi-pass door hardware kits are available at most home centers and include all the parts you'll need to hang the sliding doors for this closet project. The hardware consists of a length of metal track (A) that attaches to the closet header. Roller brackets (B) fasten to the tops of the doors with screws and glide in grooves in the track. Plastic door guides (C) screw to the floor and keep the doors from swinging back and forth or colliding as they move past one another.

PHOTO K: Cut the bi-pass door tracks to length, if necessary, and install them with screws driven into the header.

front support. Fasten the track sections to the underside of the header with screws (**See Photo K**).

20 Attach the roller hardware to the doors using the screws provided in the hardware kit. Follow the manufacturer's instructions carefully; the roller brackets are offset at two different distances to allow the doors to slide past one another. Install the finger pulls.

21 Hang the doors and install the door guides on the floor.

Corner China Cabinet

With its recessed soffit and decorative—but very functional—plate shelf, this charming corner cabinet will fit so naturally in your dining room decor that you'll wonder how you ever got along without it. The upper section, complete with glass doors, has four generous display shelves so you can give those china heirlooms the visibility they deserve. And below, there's room for candles, placemats and other odds and ends that need tucking away. This project might stretch your woodworking skills a bit, but follow our clear drawings, photos and text to create a piece of built-in furniture that will make you proud.

Vital statistics

TYPE: Corner china cabinet

OVERALL SIZE: 38½W by 85¾H by 25¼D

MATERIAL: Red oak, red oak plywood

JOINERY: Dadoes, rabbets, butt joints and dowel joints

CONSTRUCTION DETAILS:

· Top, bottom and fixed shelf attach to back panels with dado joints reinforced with screws
· Wallboard soffit built after cabinet is installed
· Soffit structure built with cleats
· Upper and lower door joints made with matched rail and stile bits on the router table
· Upper door top rails milled with a shop-built router jig and straight bit so doors can accept rectangular glass panels

FINISH: Stain and polyurethane to match your surrounding woodwork

Building time

PREPARING STOCK: 2-4 hours

LAYOUT: 6-8 hours

CUTTING PARTS: 4-6 hours

ASSEMBLY: 6-8 hours

FINISHING: 4-6 hours

INSTALLATION: 4-6 hours

TOTAL: 26-38 hours

Shopping List

- [ ] (2) ¾ in. × 4 × 8 ft. red oak plywood
- [ ] (1) ¾ in. × 4 × 4 ft. red oak plywood
- [ ] (3) ¾ × 6 in. × 8 ft. red oak
- [ ] (6) ¾ × 3 in. × 8 ft. red oak
- [ ] (1) 4 ft. 2 × 4
- [ ] (1) ¾ × ¾ × 48 in. oak cove molding
- [ ] (1) ⁹⁄₁₆ × 2 × 48 in. oak cove molding
- [ ] (18) ⅜-dia. × 1½ in. dowel pins
- [ ] (16) ⅝-dia. × 1¼ in. oak spindles
- [ ] ¾ in. × 10 lin. ft. iron-on oak edge tape
- [ ] (1) ½ in. × 4 × 4 ft. wallboard, wallboard tape, joint compound
- [ ] (2) ⅛ × 9 × 41⅝ in. tempered glass
- [ ] (10) ⅜ in. inset brass hinges
- [ ] (4) 3½ in. brass door pulls
- [ ] (12) Adjustable shelf pins
- [ ] Wood glue
- [ ] 6d finish nails, brads
- [ ] Drywall screws (3-, 2¼-,1½-in.)
- [ ] 3 in. wall anchors
- [ ] Finishing materials

Corner China Cabinet

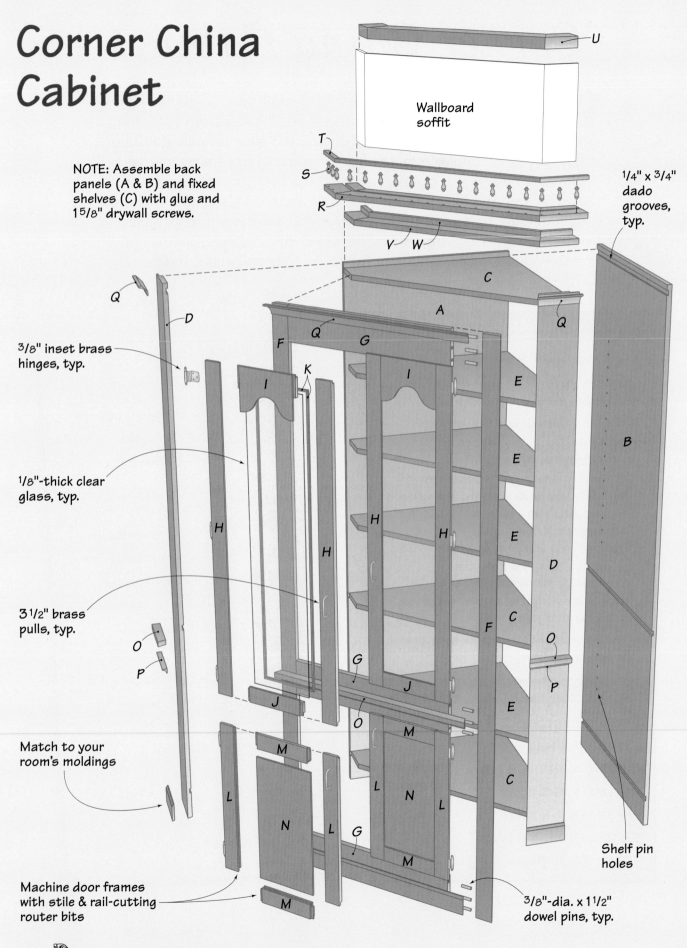

NOTE: Assemble back panels (A & B) and fixed shelves (C) with glue and 1⁵/₈" drywall screws.

Wallboard soffit

¼" x ¾" dado grooves, typ.

³/₈" inset brass hinges, typ.

¹/₈"-thick clear glass, typ.

3¹/₂" brass pulls, typ.

Match to your room's moldings

Machine door frames with stile & rail-cutting router bits

Shelf pin holes

³/₈"-dia. x 1¹/₂" dowel pins, typ.

4 Make the top, bottom and fixed shelf. Since all three of these panels are the same size, use the *Top, Bottom & Fixed Shelf* drawing on page 130 to lay out one of these parts carefully—you'll use it as a pattern for drawing the shapes of the other two parts without measuring. Note that the grain runs across these pieces, parallel to the front edges. Cut out the shape with a circular saw guided against a clamped straightedge, then outline its shape on ¾-in. plywood to make the other two panels, and cut them out.

5 Make the adjustable shelves. Refer to the *Adjustable Shelves* drawing, page 130, to lay out and cut one shelf to size, and use it as a template for making the other three shelves. Apply iron-on oak edge tape to the front edges of all four shelves.

6 Assemble the cabinet. First, drill pilot holes through the back panels from inside the dadoes to establish locations for screws. Then lay the left back panel flat on your worksurface and spread glue along the back edge. Clamp the right back panel in place against the glued edge of the left back panel, drill countersunk pilot holes along the back joint, and fasten the back panels together with 1½-in. drywall screws. Spread glue in the dadoes, and clamp the top, bottom and fixed shelf in place between the back panels. Drill countersunk holes at the dado reference holes you drilled at the beginning of this step, and fasten the cabinet parts together with 1½-in. drywall screws **(See Photo C)**. Note that the back panels overhang the top, bottom and fixed shelf by ¼ in. on both sides.

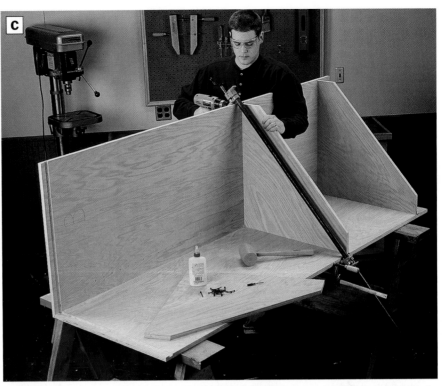

PHOTO C: Glue and screw the back panels together at the back corner joint, then spread glue in the back panel dadoes and clamp the cabinet top, bottom and fixed shelf in place. Drive screws through countersunk holes in the back panels to fasten these parts in place.

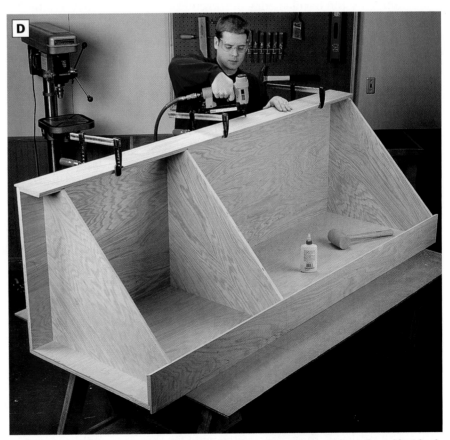

PHOTO D: Install the end pieces on the cabinet so the scribe rabbets overhang the cabinet back panels. Spread glue over the mating surfaces of the cabinet and end pieces, clamp the ends in place with the beveled edges facing inward, and fasten the ends with a nail gun or finish nails.

PHOTO E: Dry-fit the face frame stiles on the cabinet, and hold them in place with a strap clamp. Use a face frame rail to measure the amount that will need to be trimmed from the stiles to fit the rails.

PHOTO F: Drill dowel holes across the joints of the face frame rails and stiles, spread glue on the mating surfaces of the joints and dowels, and clamp up the face frame. Check it for square.

7 Attach the ends: Spread glue into the dadoes of one end piece and on the mating surfaces of the cabinet. Clamp the end in place so the scribe rabbet overhangs the back panel (take care to keep the clamps from damaging the beveled edge of the end piece). Fasten the end to the cabinet with pneumatic fasteners or finish nails. Repeat this process to attach the other end piece to the cabinet **(See Photo D)**.

BUILD & INSTALL THE FACE FRAME

The guiding principle for building the face frame is that the finished door openings must be 25 in. wide and centered on the front of the cabinet. If the openings vary from this width, the sizes of most of the door parts will need to be recalculated. Also, you'll want to create tight vertical bevel joints on the front corners of the cabinet. To accomplish these goals, cut and dry-fit the face frame parts on the cabinet before gluing the face frame together and installing it.

8 Cut the three face frame rails to size.

9 Rip and crosscut the face frame stiles, leaving them slightly wider than necessary. Bevel-rip one long edge of each stile at 22½°.

10 Dry-fit the rails and stiles on the cabinet, using a strap clamp to hold the pieces in place. Refer to the *Side Section View* drawing, page 129, for locating the rails on the stiles. If the stiles are too wide for the rails to fit, use a rail to determine the exact amount to be trimmed from the stiles **(See Photo E)**.

11 Rip an equal amount from the square edge of each stile, if trimming is necessary, to keep the door opening centered on the face frame.

12 Assemble the face frame. Mark the rail and stile joints for dowels, and use a doweling jig as a guide for drilling the ⅜-in.-dia., ¾-in.-deep dowel holes. Apply glue, insert the dowels, and clamp the frame together **(See Photo F)**.

13 Attach the face frame. Spread glue along the front edges of the cabinet, set the face frame in place and stretch broad masking tape across the bevel joints to hold them closed. Nail the face frame to the cabinet **(See Photo G)**.

FINISH THE CABINET

Finishing the cabinet now, before you install it, enables you to achieve a clean joint between wood and wall, and avoid the mess and odor of working with finishing materials in your dining room.

14 Recess all nailheads and fill the voids with wood putty. Sand the cabinet surfaces and edges smooth. Stain the cabinet inside and out to generally match the surrounding woodwork, then apply varnish.

MAKE THE SOFFIT FRAME

Most of the top back cabinet area is concealed by a wallboard soffit, which also provides a back support for plates you'll display on the plate rail. The soffit attaches to the ceiling with cleats. It is sandwiched

PHOTO G: Attach the face frame, using masking tape to hold the beveled corner joints together until the glue dries. Secure the frame to the cabinet with pneumatic fasteners or finish nails.

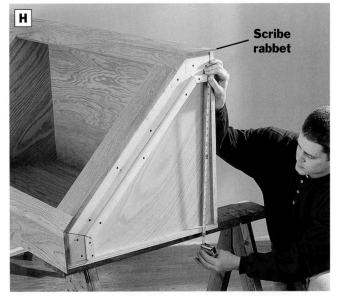

PHOTO H: Measure the distance from the cabinet soffit cleats to the cabinet back to determine the layout of the soffit cleats on the ceiling. Be sure to take into account the trimmed length of the scribe rabbets.

between the plate shelf, blocking and another cleat.

15 Stand the cabinet in position. Shim it level, and use a compass to scribe along the scribe rabbets so the cabinet will fit tightly against the wall. Trim along your scribe lines.

16 Make and attach the lower soffit cleat assembly. Cut the three sections of plate-shelf blocking and the cabinet soffit cleats to size. Miter-cut the adjoining ends so the parts fit around the inside front area of the cabinet top to form the L-shaped lower soffit cleat assembly. Attach the cleats to the blocking, then attach the blocking to the cabinet top with screws.

17 Measure for positioning the ceiling soffit cleats. The front edges of the ceiling soffit cleats must align with the front faces of soffit cleats on the cabinet. Measure the distance from the face of the cabinet soffit cleats to the back of the cabinet, and add the width of any remaining scribe (**See Photo H**). Transfer these measurements to the ceiling, and draw reference lines for positioning the ceiling cleats.

18 Cut and fasten the soffit cleats to the ceiling. Using the ceiling outline as a guide, miter-cut the three soffit cleat sections to length. Attach the cleats to the ceiling with 2¼-in. drywall screws where you can hit joists above the ceiling, or with wall anchors where no joists are available (**See Photo I**).

PHOTO I: After drawing the soffit outline on the ceiling, cut the ceiling soffit cleat sections to size and fasten them to the ceiling with long drywall screws or wall anchors, depending on your installation area.

INSTALL THE CABINET

19 First, locate the wall studs in your installation area and mark the stud locations on the outside of the cabinet back panels. Tack ½-in.-thick scrap spacers (these may need to be thinner if scribing was done) over the stud reference lines to provide solid backing for screws that will secure the cabinet to the wall. Drill pilot holes through the back panels at the stud locations and slide the cabinet into position. Level it with shims, if necessary. Attach the cabinet to the walls by driving countersunk 3-in. drywall screws into the wall studs.

20 Build the soffit. Measure and cut three wallboard sections to size and attach them to the ceiling and soffit cabinet cleats with drywall screws (**See Photo J**). Apply wallboard tape and joint compound to the four vertical joints (and the ceiling line, if no ceiling cove will be used), sand the joints smooth when dry, and finish the soffit to match the adjoining walls.

MAKE THE MOLDINGS & TRIM

21 Make the spindle rail: Rip a 4-ft.-long piece of ¾-in. oak to ½ in. thick and sand the surfaces smooth. Mark the spindle hole positions, 2½ in. apart and centered on the width of the rail (See *Layout: Spindles,* page 130). Verify the diameter and depth of the holes required by the spindles you have purchased—ours called for a ¼-in.-dia. hole in the rail and a ⁵⁄₁₆-in.-dia. hole in the plate shelf. Drill the spindle holes on a drill press or with a doweling jig. Glue the spindles to the rail.

22 Make the plate shelf: Rip the shelf to width, and cut the ½-in-wide, ⅜-in.-deep plate rim groove with your router and straight bit or a table saw and dado blade. Cut the three shelf pieces to length. To ensure a tight fit at the walls, cut the center section of shelf first, miter-cut the ends and set it in place on the cabinet. Verify the lengths of the short plate shelf pieces by measuring from the ends of the center section to the walls. Cut the short plate shelf pieces. Set the plate rail sections together on your worksurface.

23 Attach the spindle rail to the plate shelf. Cut the

PHOTO J: Make the soffit by cutting wallboard sections and installing them with screws driven into the cabinet and ceiling soffit cleats. Conceal the joints with wallboard tape and joint compound.

PHOTO K: After test-fitting the spindle rail sections on the three plate shelf pieces, apply glue to the spindle tenons and insert the spindles into the holes in the plate shelf. Tap the parts home with a mallet.

PHOTO L: With the plate shelf installed, cut, fit and attach the pre-finished top cove sections with pneumatic fasteners or finish nails. Cut the mitered ends of the cove carefully to make tight-fitting joints.

three spindle rail sections to length with adjoining ends mitered at 22½°. Refer to the *Layout: Spindles* drawing, page 130, for cutting the spindle rail sections so the spindles lay out correctly on the plate shelf and the centerlines are set back ⅜ in. from the front of the shelf. Mark the spindle locations on the plate shelf, and drill the spindle holes. Attach the spindle rail pieces to the shelf sections with glue **(See Photo K)**.

㉔ Finish the moldings and trim. Sand, stain and topcoat the spindle rail and plate shelf. Finish the stock you'll use for making the center cap and cove, as well as the top cove pieces.

INSTALL THE MOLDINGS & TRIM

㉕ Install the plate shelf and top cove. Fasten the shelf sections to the plate shelf blocking with finish nails or 1½-in. drywall screws. Cut the top cove sections to length, miter-cut the adjacent ends of the molding and fasten it beneath the plate shelf overhang with a nail gun or finish nails **(See Photo L)**.

㉖ Install the center cap and cove. Miter-cut the center cap sections first to fit around the cabinet, and fasten them in place on the cabinet with 6d finish nails so the top surface of the cap is 30 in. from the floor. Miter-cut the center cove sections to length and fasten them beneath the center cap with finish nails.

BUILD THE DOORS

We used matched coping-and-sticking bits in the router table to cut the door joints (See *Coping & Sticking Router Bits*, next page). If you choose to build the doors with mortise-and-tenon joints instead, verify before cutting your parts that the length of the tenons and the depth of the panel grooves remain ⅜ in. Otherwise you'll need to change the lengths of the rails and widths of the door panels.

㉗ Make the door rail blanks. Choose straight-grained oak lumber of consistent thickness. Rip stock 6 in. wide for the two upper door top rails, and 2¼ in. wide for the rest of the upper and lower door rails. Crosscut the rails precisely to length.

㉘ Cope the rails. Install the coping bit in your router table and adjust it for height, checking your set-up on scrap wood first. Attach a wooden auxiliary fence to the router table miter gauge, long enough to back up the cope cuts and to minimize bit tearout. Hold each rail facedown and firmly against the miter

PHOTO M: Cut coped profiles (See also top photo, next page) on the ends of the door rails at the router table. Register the ends of the rails with the coping bit by holding the rails against a stopblock clamped to the auxiliary fence on the miter gauge.

PHOTO N: Mill sticking profiles along one long edge of each door stile and one long edge of each rail with a stile-cutting bit. Clamp featherboards to the router table fence and table to help control the cuts.

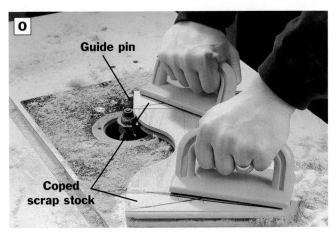

PHOTO O: Rout sticking into the arches of the upper door top rails. First remove the router fence and insert a guide pin in the router table. Fit pieces of coped scrap stock into the ends of the rails to help minimize tearout as the bit enters and exits the cuts. Then slide each rail along the guide pin so it follows the arch as you feed the rail into the bit. Use foam-soled push pads to hold the rail securely.

COPING & STICKING ROUTER BITS

Rail   Stile

Coping bit | Sticking bit

Coping and sticking router bits are used to shape the joints and inside edges of a frame for a frame-and-panel door. The set shown here consists of a "coping bit", used to profile the ends of the door rails. A "sticking bit" cuts a complementary profile in the door stiles so they interlock with the coped ends of the rails, forming the corner frame joints. Sticking is routed along the full inside edge of the stiles as well as the inside edge of the rails, creating a profiled recess for glass or a wood panel.

PHOTO P: Apply glue to the rail and stile joints, assemble the door frames with the lower door panels in place, and clamp up both sets of doors. Check the doors for square by measuring their diagonals.

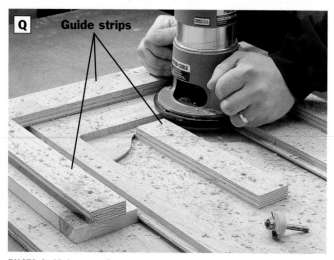

PHOTO Q: Make room for a rectangular pane of glass in the arched doors by removing excess wood in the back of the arch with a router and straight bit. Build a plywood jig to hold the doors securely. Fasten guide strips to the jig to limit the router's cutting area on the door. A center guide strip provides additional support for the router base.

fence as you cope both ends (**See Photo M**).

29 Cut the sticking on the stiles and rails. Install and adjust the sticking bit in the router table. Rip stock for the stiles from straight-grained oak, and cut the eight door stiles to length. Clamp featherboards to your router fence and router table to help you control the workpieces as you rout the sticking profiles. Mill the sticking profile along one edge of each stile (**See Photo N**) and the inside edge of the six narrow rails. Make these cuts with the parts facedown.

30 Lay out the arches on the two upper door top rails, using the *Upper Door Top Rails* drawing, page 131, to draw the shapes. Cut out the arches with a jig saw and sand the curved edges smooth.

31 Cut the sticking profiles along the arches of the upper door top rails. Although you'll use the same bit height setting in Step 29, you'll need to remove the router fence and install a guide pin in the router table to mill these curved edges (**See Photo O**). NOTE: *A guide pin provides support for contoured workpieces as you feed them into the bit.*

32 Make the lower door panels. Cut the panels to size from ¼-in. oak plywood, then dry-fit the lower door parts together to check the fit.

33 Assemble the door frames. Dry-fit them first, then spread glue in the cope joints, taking care to keep glue out of the panel grooves in the lower doors so the panels can "float". Clamp the doors together in pairs, and check them for square by measuring from corner to corner. Adjust the clamps if necessary to make them square (**See Photo P**).

34 Mill a ⅜-in. roundover along the front long outside edges of the door stiles, opposite the sticking edge. Then cut a ⅜-in. rabbet into the back long outside edges of the door stiles and the top and bottom inside edges of the door rails so the doors will overlay the face frame openings once installed. NOTE: *You could accomplish both of these milling procedures at once, if desired, by using a door lip bit in the router table instead.*

35 Rabbet the back inside edges of the upper door frames to form recesses for glass. Use a piloted ⅜-in. rabbeting bit to mill these profiles.

36 Square up the glass recesses behind the upper

door arches. In order to buy rectangular glass panes for these doors, you'll need to remove a squared-off area of material behind the door arches. We used a router and straight bit to accomplish this task. Build a plywood jig to hold each door in place, and attach guide strips around the jig to limit the path of the router base as you hog out the waste in the door arch area. The exact locations of these guide strips will depend on the size of your router base and the bit diameter you use. Regardless, the guide strips should stop the router bit 3⅛ in. in from the top end of each door and align the bit cuts with the rabbets you milled for the glass. Attach another strip of plywood in the center area of the jig to provide additional support for the router base. Mount a straight-cutting bit in your router and set the bit depth at ⅜ in. Set each door facedown in the jig, and rout the glass openings square (**See Photo Q**).

37 Rip and crosscut the glass retainer strips to fit around the inside back rabbets of the upper doors.

38 Sand the four cabinet doors and retainer strips smooth. Stain and topcoat these parts.

39 Install the glass panes. Lay the glass panes in place in the upper doors and install the retainer strips with ¾-in. brads, driven into angled pilot holes. Set the nailheads below the surface and conceal them with tinted wood putty (**See Photo R**).

FINISHING TOUCHES

40 Install the doors with ⅜-in. brass inset hinges. Mount the hinges on the doors, using three hinges for each upper door and two hinges on the lower doors. Attach the hinges to the doors first, positioning the hinges 2 in. from the top and bottom edges of the doors. Center the third hinge top-to-bottom on the upper doors. Position the doors in their openings on the cabinet. Mark the screw locations on the face frame, drill pilot holes for the screws and install the doors on the cabinet (**See Photo S**).

41 Install the door pulls. Set the handles 1 in. in from the inside edges of the doors. We positioned the upper door pulls 16 in. up from the bottom ends of the doors. The lower door pulls are mounted 2 in. below the tops of the doors.

42 Install the shelf pins and adjustable shelves. Install baseboard molding around the cabinet base to match your existing room molding.

PHOTO R: Insert the glass into the upper doors, slip the glass retainer strips into place and attach them with ¾-in. brads driven into pilot holes. Protect the glass with a piece of cardboard when you tap the brads into place.

PHOTO S: Attach the hinges to the doors, set the doors into place on the cabinet, and mark the hinge screw locations on the face frame. Drill pilot holes and drive in the hinge screws to hang the doors.

Home Theater

This stylish built-in unit is much more than a place to put your TV—it's a professional-quality home for all of your state-of-the-art home entertainment components. Install your audio components, slide the TV, VCR and center-channel speaker into their places, arrange the surround speakers and subwoofer and you're ready to invite your friends over for the big game or the latest video release. Deceptively simple in appearance, this birch and black melamine project is more complex than it appears, but the payoff for careful craftsmanship is obvious—its sleek, modern styling and delicate reveals will make it the focal point of any room.

Vital statistics

TYPE: Home theater

OVERALL SIZE: 83¼L by 94½H by 25½D

MATERIAL: Birch plywood and lumber, black melamine

JOINERY: Butt joints reinforced with screws

CONSTRUCTION DETAILS:
- Frameless cabinet box construction
- Part edges are concealed with solid-wood nosing or birch edge tape
- Most nosing edges eased with ¼-in. roundover
- Fully concealed hinges on doors
- Roll-out shelves are outfitted with full-extension drawer slides
- Visible parts are separated by ⅛ in. spacers to produce consistent reveals

FINISH: Polyurethane

Building time

PREPARING STOCK: 5-7 hours

LAYOUT: 4-6 hours

CUTTING PARTS: 10-12 hours

ASSEMBLY: 12-16 hours

FINISHING: 4-6 hours

INSTALLATION: 8-13 hours

TOTAL: 43-60 hours

Shopping List

- ☐ (5) ¾ in. × 4 × 8 ft. birch plywood
- ☐ (7) ¾ in. × 4 × 8 ft. black melamine
- ☐ (1) ⅛ in. × 4 × 4 ft. hardboard
- ☐ (3) ¾ × 1½ in. × 8 ft. birch
- ☐ (12) Double-roller friction catches
- ☐ Black speaker cloth, 6 sq. ft.
- ☐ ¾ in. birch edge tape (70 lin. ft.)
- ☐ ¾ in. black edge tape (150 lin. ft.)
- ☐ (16) Euro-style hinges (clip-on, snap-closing, 125° opening)
- ☐ (8) 3½ in. wire door pulls (chrome)
- ☐ (2 pair) 22-in. full-extension drawer slides (side-mounted)
- ☐ (36) Adjustable shelf pins
- ☐ Door cushions, black plastic screw caps
- ☐ Wood glue
- ☐ ¾ in. brads
- ☐ Drywall screws (1¼-, 1½-, 3¼-in.)
- ☐ Brass flathead wood screws (1½-in.)
- ☐ Finishing materials

Home Theater

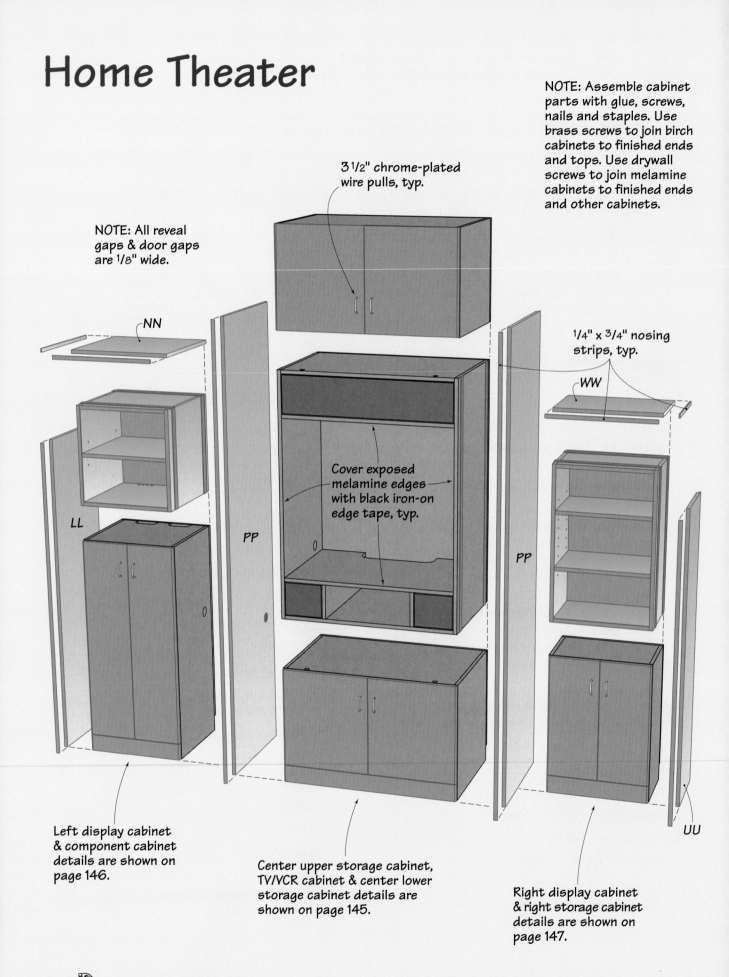

NOTE: Assemble cabinet parts with glue, screws, nails and staples. Use brass screws to join birch cabinets to finished ends and tops. Use drywall screws to join melamine cabinets to finished ends and other cabinets.

3 1/2" chrome-plated wire pulls, typ.

NOTE: All reveal gaps & door gaps are 1/8" wide.

NN

1/4" x 3/4" nosing strips, typ.

WW

Cover exposed melamine edges with black iron-on edge tape, typ.

LL

PP

PP

UU

Left display cabinet & component cabinet details are shown on page 146.

Center upper storage cabinet, TV/VCR cabinet & center lower storage cabinet details are shown on page 145.

Right display cabinet & right storage cabinet details are shown on page 147.

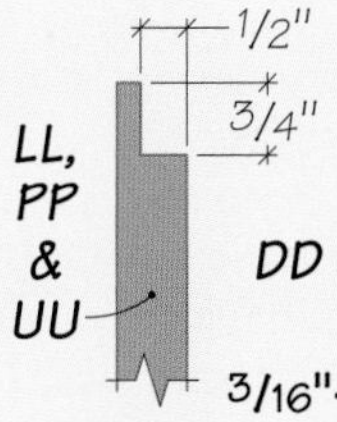

SCRIBE RABBETS

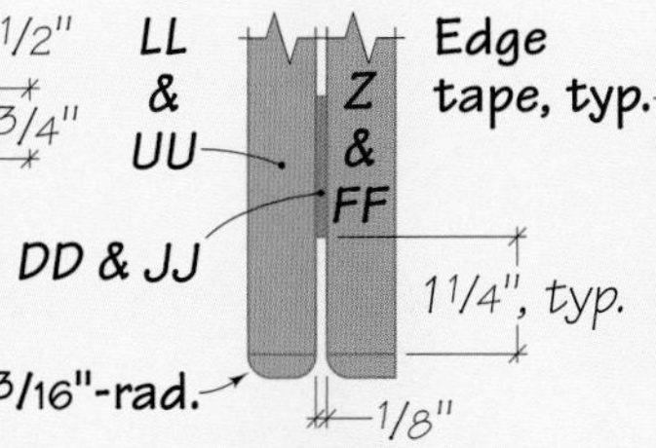

DISPLAY CABINETS

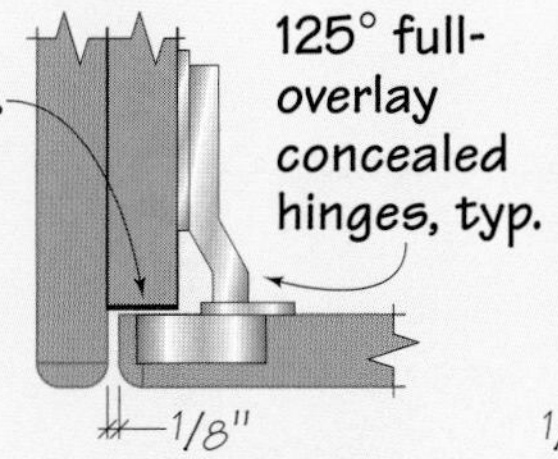

STORAGE CABINETS

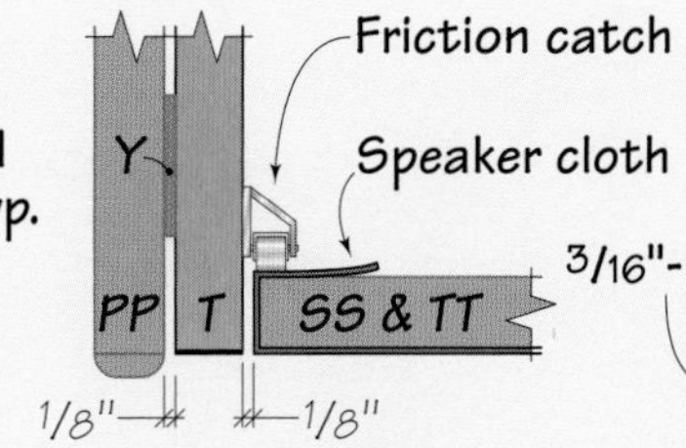

TV/VCR CABINET

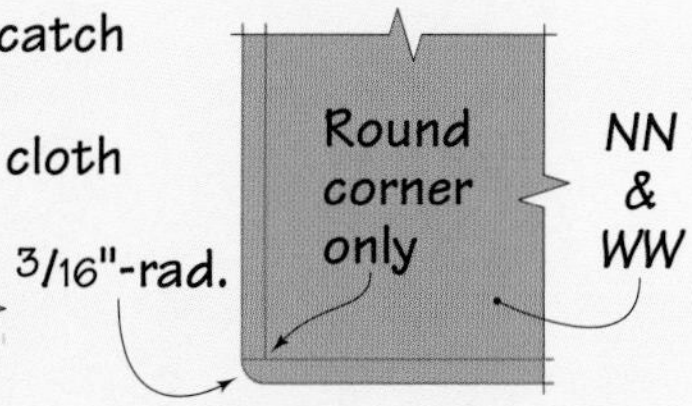

DISPLAY CABINETS FINISHED TOPS

Home Theater Cutting List

Part	No.	Size	Material
Cabinet Boxes			
COMPONENT CABINET			
A. Sides	2	¾ × 18 11/16 × 46⅛ in.	Black melamine
B. Top/bottom	2	¾ × 18 11/16 × 19¾ in.	"
C. Back	1	¾ × 21¼ × 42⅞ in.	"
D. Shelves	4	¾ × 18 9/16 × 19½ in.	"
CENTER LOWER STORAGE CABINET			
E. Sides	2	¾ × 23 3/16 × 24 in.	Black melamine
F. Top/bottom	2	¾ × 23 3/16 × 36¼ in.	"
G. Back	1	¾ × 20¾ × 37¾ in.	"
H. RO shelf spacers	4	¾ × 3¾ × 23 in.	"
I. RO shelf sides	4	¾ × 3 × 22 in.	"
J. RO shelf ends	4	¾ × 3 × 32¼ in.	"
K. RO shelf bottoms	2	¾ × 22 × 33¾ in.	"
CENTER UPPER STORAGE CABINET			
L. Sides	2	¾ × 23 3/16 × 20⅜ in.	Black melamine
M. Top/bottom	2	¾ × 23 3/16 × 36¼ in.	"
N. Back	1	¾ × 20⅜ × 37¾ in.	"
O. Shelf	1	¾ × 23 13/16 × 36 in.	"
RIGHT STORAGE CABINET			
P. Sides	2	¾ × 12 11/16 × 28½ in.	Black melamine
Q. Top/bottom	2	¾ × 12 11/16 × 19¾ in.	"
R. Back	1	¾ × 21¼ × 25¼ in.	"
S. Shelf	1	¾ × 12 9/16 × 19½ in.	"
TV/VCR CABINET			
T. Sides	2	¾ × 23¾ × 50⅛ in.	Black melamine
U. Top/bottom/shelf	3	¾ × 23¾ × 36 in.	"
V. Upper shelf	1	¾ × 18 × 36 in.	"
W. Back	1	¾ × 37½ × 50⅛ in.	"
X. Shelf supports	2	¾ × 7 × 23¾ in.	"
Y. Side spacers	4	⅛ × 1½ × 50⅛ in.	Hardboard

Part	No.	Size	Material
LEFT DISPLAY CABINET			
Z. Sides	2	¾ × 19¼ × 21 in.	Birch plywood
AA. Top/bottom	2	¾ × 19¼ × 19½ in.	"
BB. Back	1	¾ × 21 × 21 in.	"
CC. Shelf	1	¾ × 19⅜ × 19⅜ in.	"
DD. Side spacers	4	⅛ × 1½ × 21 in.	Hardboard
DD. Top spacers	2	⅛ × 1½ ×21¼ in.	"
RIGHT DISPLAY CABINET			
FF. Sides	2	¾ × 13¼ × 31⅝ in.	Birch plywood
GG. Top/bottom	2	¾ × 13¼ × 19½ in.	"
HH. Back	1	¾ × 21 × 31⅝ in.	"
II. Shelves	2	¾ × 13⅜ × 19⅜ in.	"
JJ. Side spacers	4	⅛ × 1½ × 31⅝ in.	Hardboard
KK. Top spacers	2	⅛ × 1½ ×21¼ in.	"
Exterior Parts			
LEFT UNIT			
LL. Finished end	1	¾ × 20¾ × 67⅛ in.	Birch plywood
MM. Doors	2	¾ × 10 3/16 × 42⅜ in.	"
NN. Top	1	¾ × 20¾ × 21¾ in.	"
OO. Baseboard	1	¾ × 3½ × 20½ in.	"
CENTER UNIT			
PP. Finished ends	2	¾ × 25¼ × 94½ in.	Birch plywood
QQ. Doors	4	¾ × 18 7/16 × 20¼ in.	"
RR. Baseboard	1	¾ × 3½ × 37 in.	"
SS. Speaker panel	1	¾ × 7⅝ × 35⅝ in.	"
TT. Small fabric panels	2	¾ × 6⅝ × 7⅞ in.	"
RIGHT UNIT			
UU. Finished end	1	¾ × 14¾ × 60⅛ in.	Birch plywood
VV. Doors	2	¾ × 10 3/16 × 24¾ in.	"
WW. Top	1	¾ × 14¾ × 21¾ in.	"
XX. Baseboard	1	¾ × 3½ × 20½ in.	"

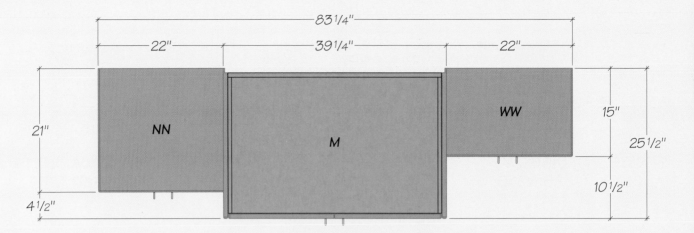

83¼"

22" 39¼" 22"

NN

M

WW

21"

15"

25½"

10½"

4½"

TOP VIEW

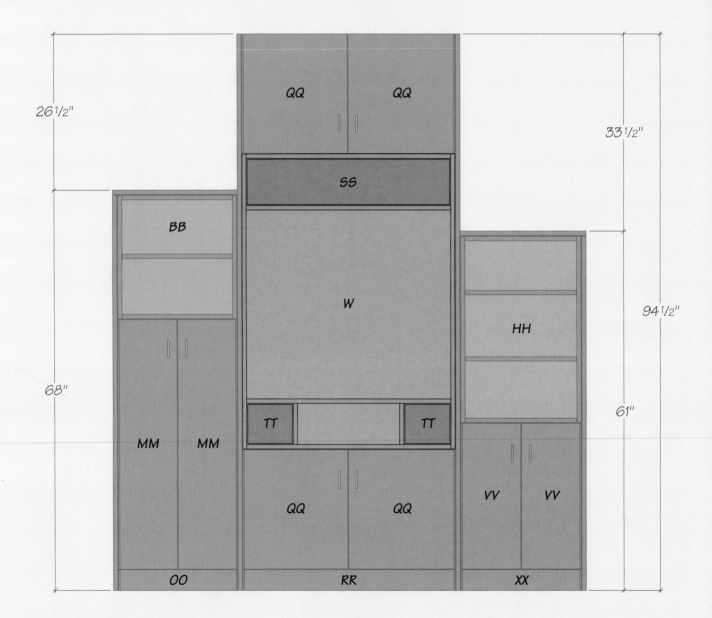

26½"

QQ QQ

SS

BB

33½"

W

HH

94½"

68"

MM MM

TT TT

61"

QQ QQ

VV VV

OO RR XX

FRONT VIEW

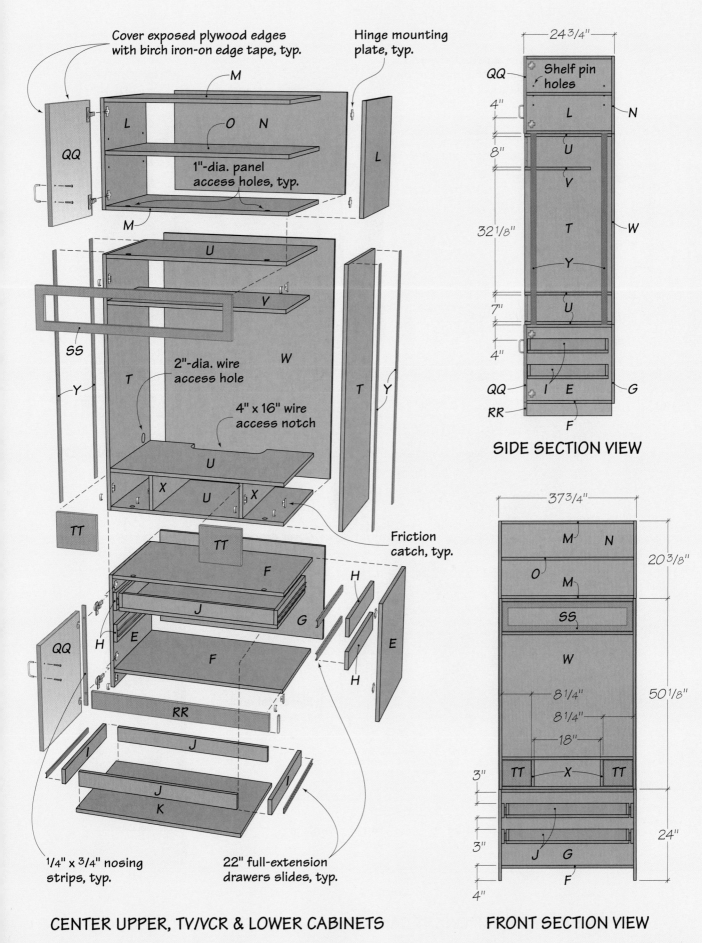

Cover exposed plywood edges with birch iron-on edge tape, typ.

Hinge mounting plate, typ.

M

L

QQ

O   N

L

1"-dia. panel access holes, typ.

M

24 3/4"

QQ

Shelf pin holes

4"

L

N

8"

U

V

32 1/8"

T

W

Y

7"

U

4"

QQ

I   E

G

RR

F

SIDE SECTION VIEW

U

V

SS

Y

T

2"-dia. wire access hole

W

T   Y

4" x 16" wire access notch

U

X   U   X

TT

Friction catch, typ.

TT

F

H

J

H   G

QQ

H

E   E

H

F

RR

J

I

J

K

I

1/4" x 3/4" nosing strips, typ.

22" full-extension drawers slides, typ.

37 3/4"

M   N

20 3/8"

O   M

SS

W

50 1/8"

8 1/4"

8 1/4"

18"

3"

TT   X   TT

3"

J   G

24"

F

4"

FRONT SECTION VIEW

CENTER UPPER, TV/VCR & LOWER CABINETS

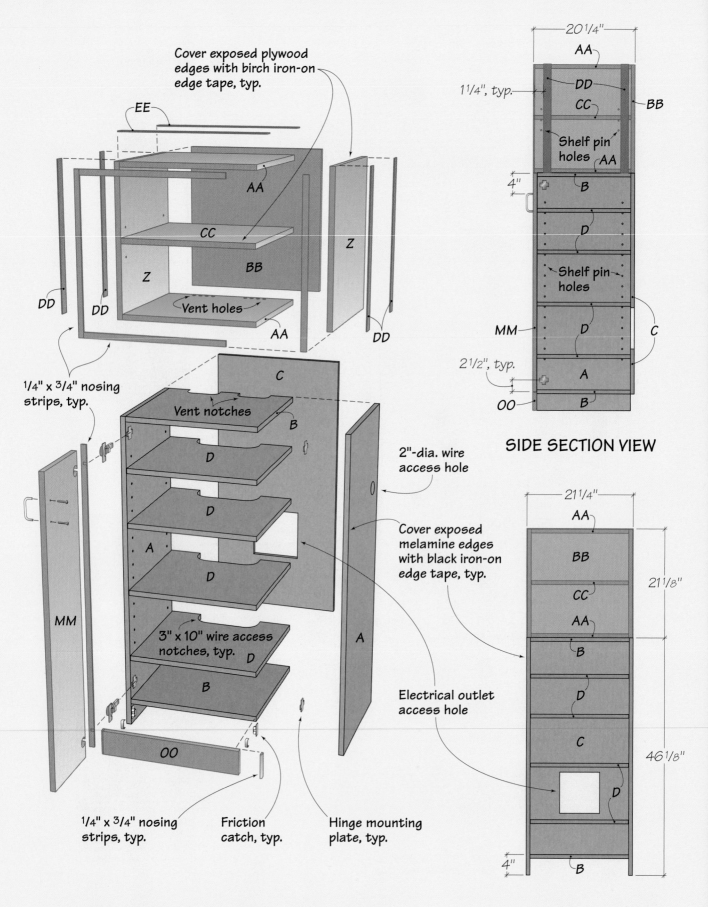

Cover exposed plywood edges with birch iron-on edge tape, typ.

EE

AA

CC

BB

Z

Z

DD

DD

DD

DD

Vent holes

AA

1/4" x 3/4" nosing strips, typ.

20 1/4"

AA

1 1/4", typ.

DD

CC

BB

Shelf pin holes

AA

4"

B

D

Shelf pin holes

D

MM

C

2 1/2", typ.

A

OO

B

SIDE SECTION VIEW

C

Vent notches

B

D

D

D

A

D

2"-dia. wire access hole

Cover exposed melamine edges with black iron-on edge tape, typ.

3" x 10" wire access notches, typ.

D

MM

A

B

OO

Electrical outlet access hole

1/4" x 3/4" nosing strips, typ.

Friction catch, typ.

Hinge mounting plate, typ.

21 1/4"

AA

BB

CC

21 1/8"

AA

B

D

C

D

46 1/8"

4"

B

LEFT DISPLAY & COMPONENT CABINETS

FRONT SECTION VIEW

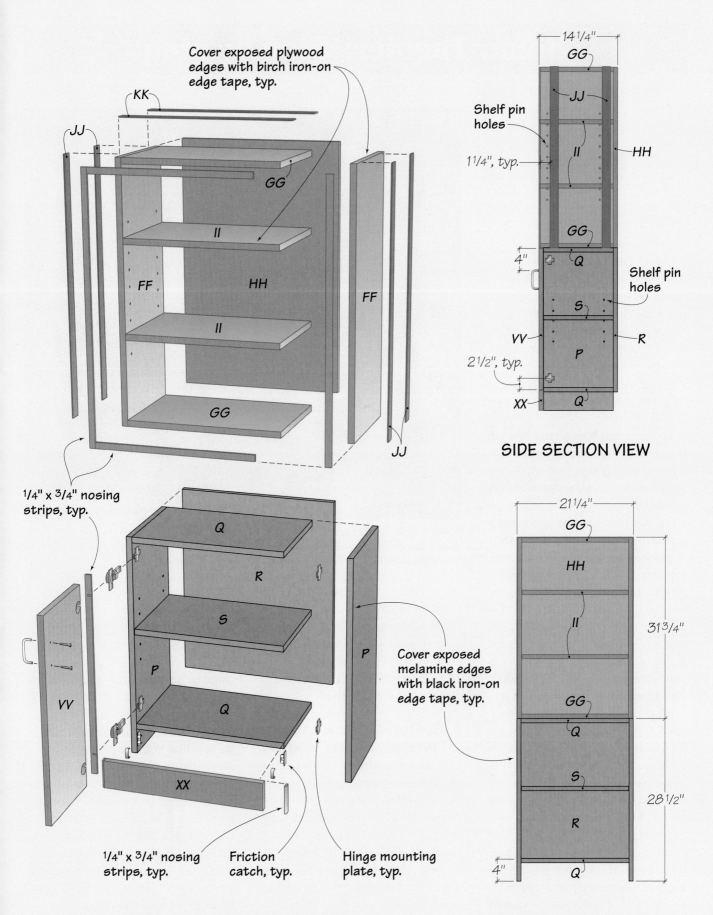

Cover exposed plywood edges with birch iron-on edge tape, typ.

KK

JJ

GG

FF

HH

FF

II

II

GG

JJ

¼" x ¾" nosing strips, typ.

SIDE SECTION VIEW

14¼"

GG

JJ

Shelf pin holes

1¼", typ.

II

HH

GG

4"

Q

Shelf pin holes

S

VV

R

2½", typ.

P

XX

Q

Q

R

S

P

P

VV

¼" x ¾" nosing strips, typ.

XX

Friction catch, typ.

Hinge mounting plate, typ.

Cover exposed melamine edges with black iron-on edge tape, typ.

FRONT SECTION VIEW

21¼"

GG

HH

II

GG

Q

S

R

Q

31¾"

28½"

4"

RIGHT DISPLAY & STORAGE CABINETS

GENERAL NOTES

The cabinets in this project (sometimes called "European style") do not have face frames like traditional American cabinets. Without face frames, the hinges mount to the door backs and to the inside walls of the cabinet so they are fully concealed when the doors are closed.

Accuracy in measuring and cutting parts is extremely important when building this project, because ⅛-in. reveals between the cabinets leave nowhere to hide irregularities. The reveals become a subtle decorative element, and it is quite noticeable if they are not consistent. NOTE: *The shelf and cabinet dimensions in this project are sized according to standard or average electronic components. If you already own electronic equipment, measure the actual sizes of your components before you start building, and adjust accordingly.*

This project is built entirely from sheet goods. The interior cabinet boxes are made of black melamine and clad with birch outer parts. The display cabinets, finished ends and baseboards are made of ¾-in. birch plywood. The exposed part edges will be either covered with nosing or edge tape. Solid ¼-in.-thick birch nosing is applied whenever part edges will be rounded. Most square exposed edges will receive iron-on birch

PHOTO A: Apply black edge tape to the front edges of the melamine cabinet box parts, using a household iron. While the adhesive is still soft, roll the banding firmly with a J-roller to secure the bond. Trim the edges with an edge trimmer or sharp utility knife.

veneer edge tape instead.

It is easiest to assemble these large cabinets on a broad platform, rather than a workbench or the floor. The ideal platform is 18 to 30 in. high, 4 ft. × 6 ft., sturdy, level and smooth.

BUILD THE FOUR MELAMINE INTERIOR CABINET BOXES

The interior cabinet boxes include the left component cabinet, the center upper storage cabinet, the center lower storage cabinet and the right storage cabinet. The interior boxes are built entirely of ¾-in. black melamine and then clad with birch exterior parts in the completed project. The building process is identical for all four

cabinets, so you might think it would be most efficient to cut all the parts at once, apply all the edgebanding and then assemble the four cabinets. However, this approach also carries the greatest risk of compounding minor errors which may not be noticed until later. Unless you are experienced in building similar cabinetry, we recommend cutting the parts for one cabinet at a time, then assembling each cabinet before moving on to the next cabinet. Also, at this stage, build just the cabinet boxes and adjustable shelves. You'll build and install the roll-out shelves later, after the doors have been fitted and the hinges installed.

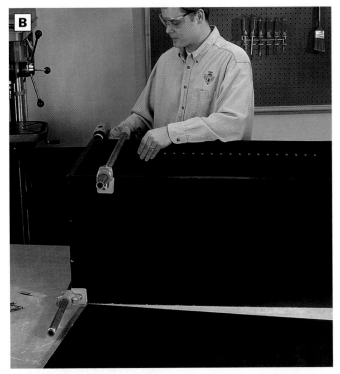

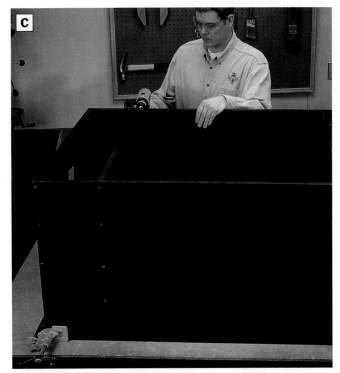

PHOTO B: After drilling the adjustable shelf pin holes, assemble each cabinet by clamping the top and bottom in place, drilling countersunk pilot holes, and driving 1½-in. drywall screws. The cabinet backs, once installed, will hold the cabinet boxes square.

PHOTO C: Hold the narrow upper shelf flush with the TV/VCR cabinet face to create air flow space behind it. Clamp the shelf in position, drill countersunk pilot holes and fasten with drywall screws.

❶ Make the parts for the component cabinet. Cut the sides, top, bottom, back, and four shelves to size. Lay out the vent and wire access notches in the top and shelves (See *Left Display & Component Cabinets* drawing, page 146) and cut them out with your jig saw. Apply black edge tape to the front edges of the sides, top, bottom and shelves **(See Photo A)**. Also apply edge tape to the top edges of the sides and back, which may be slightly visible in the finished project.

❷ Drill the cabinet sides for adjustable shelf pins. Make a drilling template from ¼-in. hardboard to ensure that the holes are aligned and evenly spaced. Drill both rows of holes in each side, spacing the holes 2 in. apart.

❸ Assemble the cabinet. Clamp the top and bottom in position between the sides and secure the parts with countersunk 1½-in. drywall screws **(See Photo B)**. Position the back, using it to square up the cabinet box, and attach the back with screws.

❹ Build the center upper and lower storage cabinets as well as the right storage cabinet using the same procedure as outlined for the left component cabinet. Again, assemble these cabinets one at a time.

BUILD THE TV/VCR CABINET

The TV/VCR cabinet is also built of melamine, but it will not be concealed by doors when the project is done.

❺ Make the cabinet parts. Cut the sides, top, bottom, back, shelves and shelf supports to size. Cut out the wire access notch in the back edge of the lower shelf with your jig saw. Apply black edge tape to the front edges of all the parts.

❻ Build the lower shelf assembly with its VCR compartment. Position the shelf spacers 8¼ in. in from the side edges of the cabinet bottom and lower shelf. Drill countersunk pilot holes and fasten the spacers to the bottom and shelf with drywall screws.

❼ Build the cabinet. Clamp the lower shelf assembly, the upper shelf and the cabinet top in position between the sides with the front edges of the parts held flush. Drill countersunk pilot holes and fasten the parts together with 1½-in. drywall screws **(See Photo C)**. Position the cabinet back, using it to square up the cabinet box. Drill countersunk pilot holes and attach the back with screws.

❽ Attach the side spacers. The purpose of the spac-

PHOTO D: The hardboard spacer strips create a ⅛-in. reveal between the TV/VCR cabinet and the finished end. Inset the spacers 1¼ in. from the front and back edges of the cabinet. Attach the spacers with ¾-in. brads.

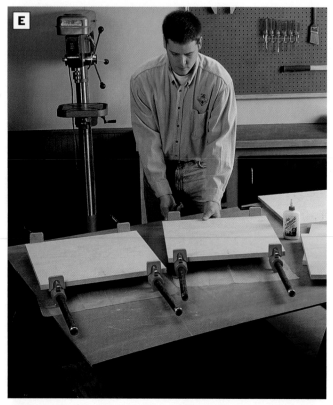

PHOTO E: Glue ¼-in. birch nosing to the leading edges of the display cabinet sides, tops and bottoms. Glue and clamp them in place.

ers is to create ⅛-in. reveals between the sides of the TV/VCR cabinet and the birch finished ends, matching the other reveals in the project. The spacers will be nearly invisible in the completed project, so you may combine shorter strips if that enables you to make better use of materials. Locate the spacer strips 1¼ in. in from the front and back edges of the cabinet. If desired, the front edge of the front spacer can be blackened with magic marker or paint to help hide it. Cut the spacers to size and attach them with ¾-in. brads (**See Photo D**).

BUILD THE DISPLAY CABINETS

❾ Make the parts. Cut out the tops, bottoms, sides, backs and shelves from birch plywood. Follow the *Cutting List* dimensions carefully for cutting these parts—the display cabinets differ in height and depth. Drill a row of ½-in.-dia. holes in the bottom of the left display cabinet for air circulation (See *Left Display & Component Cabinets,* page 146). Use a template to drill shelf pin holes in the sides. Apply birch edge tape to the front edges of the shelves and the top edges of the sides. Rip and crosscut strips of ¼-in.-thick, ¾-in.-wide solid birch nosing and apply it to the front edges of the side, top and bottom panels with glue and clamps (**See Photo E**).

❿ Assemble the cabinets. Spread glue on the edges of the tops and bottoms, and clamp them in place between the sides. Drill countersunk pilot holes, and fasten the cabinets together with 1½-in. drywall screws (**See Photo F**). Attach the backs with glue and countersunk screws.

⓫ Round-over the outside edges of the nosing on the cabinet sides. Use a router and piloted 3/16-in. round-over bit to shape these edges (**See Photo G**).

⓬ Rip and crosscut pairs of hardboard spacer strips to wrap around the sides and tops of both cabinets. Hold the spacers 1½ in. from the front edges of the cabinets and 1¼ in. from the backs. Attach the spacers with ¾-in. brads (**See Photo H**).

MAKE THE EXTERIOR PARTS

All three sets of lower doors are installed directly above a baseboard. Notice in the drawings that all four sets of doors will receive nosing on the outside long edges, but the inside edges and top and bottom ends will be banded.

⓭ Cut the doors and baseboards to size. To achieve a

PHOTO F: Assemble the display cabinets by spreading glue on the edges of the tops and bottoms, clamping them in place between the sides and fastening the parts together with 1½-in. drywall screws.

PHOTO G: Use your router and a piloted ³⁄₁₆-in. roundover bit to shape the outside edges of the nosing on the display cabinet sides. Note the ½-in.-dia. air flow holes drilled through the cabinet bottom.

grain-matched effect, lay out and cut each set of doors (and baseboard) from a single plywood blank. Determine the actual widths of the doors by measuring the outside width of the cabinet boxes and subtracting ¾ in. (two ⅛-in. reveals plus two ¼-in. door nosings). NOTE: *Although this technique will produce grain match across each set of doors and between the doors and adjacent baseboards, try to keep grain pattern consistent among all four sets of doors for a pleasing wood grain effect.*

⓮ Rip, crosscut and install ¼-in.-thick birch nosing on the outer long edges of each door as well as the short ends of the baseboards.

⓯ Shape the outer front edges of the door and baseboard nosing with a router and piloted ³⁄₁₆-in. roundover bit **(See Photo I)**, taking care to keep the corners crisp and sharp. TIP: *Clamp a scrap back-up block to each end of the nosing before you start rounding over the edge to minimize bit tearout.*

⓰ Apply birch edge tape to the long inside edges of the doors (opposite the nosed edges), then cover the top and bottom door ends with edge tape to conceal the plies **(See Photo J)**. Apply edge tape to the top

PHOTO H: Staple ⅛-in. hardboard spacers to the sides and top of the display cabinets. Hold the front spacers 1¼ in. back from the front cabinet face.

PHOTO I: Rout a ³⁄₁₆-in. roundover on the outer front edge of the door nosing. You may want to clamp back-up blocks at the ends of the nosing (not shown in photo) to avoid accidentally rounding the corners.

PHOTO J: Apply birch edge tape to the other long edges of the doors with an iron on low heat. Then apply banding to both ends. Trim the banding flush with an edge trimmer or sharp utility knife.

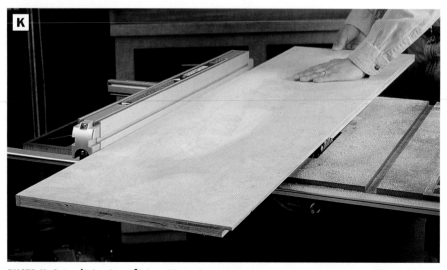

PHOTO K: Cut a ½-in.-deep, ¾-in.-wide scribe rabbet along the back long edges of the finished ends. Make these cuts on the table saw with a dado blade.

long edges of the baseboards also.

17 Make finished ends for the left, center and right units. Cut the four plywood blanks to size and apply birch nosing to the front edge of each blank. Cover the top edge of the two shorter finished ends with edge tape. Use a dado blade in your table saw to cut a ½-in.-deep, ¾-in.-wide rabbet along the back edge of each of the four finished ends **(See Photo K)**. Removing the waste simplifies scribing the panels for a flush installation (For more on scribing, see page 15). Shape both long edges of the nosing on these parts with your router and a ³⁄₁₆-in. piloted roundover bit.

18 Make the two display cabinet tops. Cut the plywood blanks to size, and apply nosing to the front and outer edges only. Round-over the nosed corner of each top so it will align with the roundover profile of the finished end below it. We used a scrap with a routed edge for reference, and rounded the corners with a file and sandpaper **(See Photo L)**.

MOUNT THE DOORS & BASEBOARDS

Mount the doors and baseboards onto the cabinets before finishing and installing them. Remove the doors for finishing and re-mount them after the cabinets have been installed. We used clip-on, snap-closing Euro-style hinges that have mounting plates designed for easy door attachment and removal. Read and follow the hinge manufacturer's instructions for installing the hinge hardware. Because it's important for the doors to overlap the front edges of the cabinet sides by ⅝ in. (leaving a ⅛-in. reveal between the door and the finished end), test the hinge cup placement on plywood scraps to confirm the correct left-right centerline before boring cup holes into the actual doors.

⑲ Drill hinge cups in the doors. Clamp a scrap fence to your drill press table and position it so the drill bit will be properly inset from the back edge of each door as you drill the hinge cup holes. Mark the drill bit centerline on top of the fence for reference. Locate the vertical center of the hinge cup holes 2½ in. from the top and bottom ends of each door. Follow the manufacturer's guidelines for hole diameter and depth. With a door clamped firmly in place, bore the two hinge cup holes **(See Photo M)**.

⑳ Install the hinge mounting plates in the cabinets. The vertical door positions are different for the center upper cabinet than for the three lower cabinets. The center upper doors are flush with the cabinet top (as well as the top edges of the applied finished ends) and they overlap the cabinet bottom by ⅝ in. The doors on the lower cabinets overlap the cabinet tops by ⅝ in. and overlap the cabinet bottoms by ⅜ in. Locate and install the mounting plates on the cabinet sides to achieve the correct door positioning.

㉑ Hang the doors. Stand each cabinet upright, then mount the doors by connecting the hinges to the hinge plates. Adjust the doors for proper alignment according to the hinge manufacturer's instructions.

㉒ Fit and install the baseboards. Position each baseboard flush with the bottom edges of the cabinet sides. This should result in a ⅛-in. reveal between the

PHOTO L: Round-over the outer corner of the finished top nosing with a file and sandpaper, using a routed edge of scrap as a reference for forming the curve. The shaped corner will align with the nosing corner of the finished end panel below it.

PHOTO M: Bore the hinge cup holes in the doors with a drill press and Forstner bit. Center each hole 2½ in. from the end of the door, and follow the manufacturer's guidelines for hole diameter and depth. As an alignment guide, clamp a fence to the drill press table.

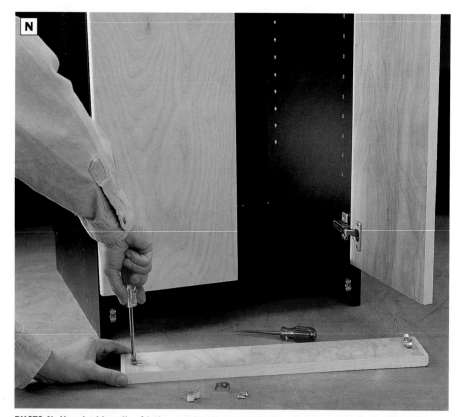

PHOTO N: Use double roller friction catches to mount the baseboard so it is flush with the bottom edges of the cabinet sides. This should result in a ⅛-in. reveal between the baseboard and the doors. The ends of the baseboard should align with the outer door edges.

PHOTO O: Install melamine spacers inside the lower cabinet for mounting the roll-out shelf slide hardware. Apply black edge tape to the top and front edges and attach the spacers with 1¼-in. drywall screws.

baseboard and the door bottoms. The ends of the baseboards should align with the door edges. Position and mount the roller catch parts inside the cabinet walls and on the back face of each baseboard **(See Photo N)**.

23 Mark and drill holes for attaching the door pulls. We mounted the pulls 4 in. down from the tops of the lower cabinet doors and 4 in. up from the bottoms of the upper center cabinet doors. The pulls are inset 1 in. from the inside edges of the doors.

FINISH THE WOOD PARTS

24 Remove the doors and baseboards from the cabinet boxes. Sand all surfaces and edges, taking care to remove any dried glue from the nosing joints. Topcoat the birch parts with polyurethane varnish.

MAKE THE ROLL-OUT SHELVES & FABRIC PANELS

25 Make and install the roll-out shelf spacers in the center lower storage cabinet. The purpose of the spacers is to protect the backs of the doors from being scratched by the metal ends of the drawer slides when the doors are opened and the shelves rolled out. Cut the spacers to size and apply edge tape to the top edges and front ends. See *Front Section View,* page 145) for positioning the four spacers inside the cabinet, and attach them with 1¼-in. drywall screws **(See Photo O)**.

26 Build the roll-out shelves. Cut the parts to size from black melamine. Clamp the ends in place between the sides, drill countersunk pilot holes, and attach the parts with 1½-in. drywall screws. Position the bottom on each shelf carcase, and use it as a reference for squaring up the assembly. Drill countersunk pilot holes through the bottom, and fasten the bottoms in place.

27 Follow the manufacturer's instructions for mounting the drawer slides on the shelf spacers and shelves. Slide the roll-out shelves into place in the cabinet, and check the shelves for smooth operation **(See Photo P)**.

28 Build and fit the three fabric panels in the TV/VCR cabinet. The long upper panel hides the center-channel speaker, and the two lower panels conceal the extra spaces on either side of the VCR compartment. The fabric panels help to visually unify the cabinet and direct the focus to the screen rather than the structure surrounding it. Confirm the panel sizes by measuring your actual openings, leaving ³⁄₁₆ in. clearance on all sides of the panel. Cut the speaker panel and two smaller fabric panels to size from ¾-in. plywood. Cut out the center of the speaker panel (and the smaller panels, if you like, for housing additional speakers), leaving a 1½-in. frame. Paint the faces black to prevent the wood from showing through the fabric. Cut speaker cloth to size, stretch it over the panels and fasten with staples **(See Photo Q)**. Mount the panels in the cabinet openings with roller friction catches, as you did for the baseboards.

INSTALL THE CABINETS

The cabinets must be installed level and plumb. Any racking of the cabinet boxes will make it nearly impossible to properly adjust the doors so the faces align with one another and with the finished ends and the baseboards. Plan to scribe and trim along the

PHOTO P: Fasten the drawer slide hardware to the roll-out shelves and the cabinet spacers, then mount the shelves in the cabinet. If your cabinet is square, the shelves should slide smoothly.

PHOTO Q: Paint the faces of the plywood fabric panels black to prevent the wood from showing through the fabric, wrap the panels in black speaker cloth and staple it in place.

PHOTO R: Drill 1-in.-dia. finger holes to provide access for popping out the fabric panels. Drill from above the upper panel and from below the lower panels, using a clamped plywood backer to prevent tearout.

PHOTO S: Clamp the birch finished end in place on the center unit with the leading edge extending ¼ in. beyond the TV/VCR cabinet. Attach the end with 1¼-in. screws driven from inside the cabinets.

scribe rabbets for a tight fit to the wall (See page 15).

29 Determine wall-stud locations and electrical outlets in your project installation area. Mark their locations on the floor or ceiling for reference.

30 Assemble the center unit. Stack the three center cabinets together with the front edges of the TV/VCR cabinet extending 9/16 in. beyond the faces of the upper and lower cabinets. Fasten the cabinets together with 1¼-in. drywall screws, driven up through the top of the cabinet below. If needed, cut an access hole in the cabinet back for reaching an electrical outlet.

31 Drill 1-in.-dia. finger holes into the fabric panel compartments about 1 in. back from the front edges for pushing the fabric panels out from behind. Drill the holes so you can access the long speaker panel from above and the smaller fabric panels from below. Clamp a scrap piece of plywood in place before you drill each hole to serve as a backer. Otherwise you'll tear out the melamine (**See Photo R**).

32 Attach the center unit finished ends. Clamp the ends in place against the stacked center cabinets. Position the ends with the nosed edges extending beyond the TV/VCR cabinet by ¼ in. and extending beyond the upper and lower cabinets by 13/16 in. Attach the ends with countersunk 1¼-in. screws driven from inside the cabinets (**See Photo S**).

33 Install the center unit on the wall. Use shims and scribe as necessary to make it level and plumb. Install the cabinet with 3¼-in. drywall screws driven through the cabinet backs and into the wall studs.

34 Assemble and install the left unit. Position and fasten the upper left display cabinet to the component cabinet so the front edges of the display cabinet extend 13/16 in. beyond the component cabinet. Drive countersunk 1¼-in. drywall screws up through the component cabinet to secure the two cabinets together. Cut an opening for the electrical outlet in the back of the component cabinet. Shim the unit as necessary to make it level and plumb and attach it to both the center unit and the wall with screws (**See Photo T**). For appearance's sake, use brass screws when fastening the upper storage cabinet to the center unit or wall, instead of drywall screws.

35 Assemble and install the right unit, following the

PHOTO T: After fastening the cabinet boxes together and cutting an opening for the electrical outlet, shim the left unit as necessary to make it level and plumb. Attach it with screws to both the wall and the center unit.

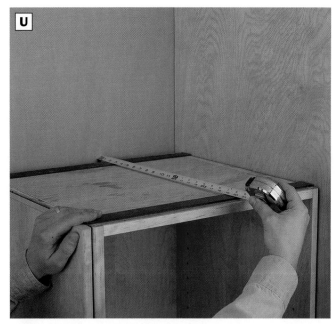

PHOTO U: With the cabinets installed, verify the final measurements of the applied tops to ensure that the front and end will be flush with the cabinets below. Trim the back edges as needed before installing them.

same basic procedure as the left unit.

36 Install the shorter finished end panels and the display cabinet tops. Attach the finished ends so the nosed edges align with the display cabinet nosing and the tops of the ends are flush with the tops of the display cabinets. Trim the scribe rabbets as necessary for a flush fit (See page 15). Verify the final measurements of the cabinet tops (**See Photo U**) and trim the back edges of the tops as needed to keep the nosed edges flush with the nosing on the display cabinets.

37 If you plan to position speakers on top of the display cabinets, drill access holes through the tops for speaker wires. Locate the holes in the back corners by the TV cabinet, and size them so you can outfit the holes with plastic grommets to protect the wires.

38 Drill holes between cabinet compartments near the back for running the necessary wires for your system (**See Photo V**).

39 Hang the doors and clip the baseboards in place. TIP: *Depending on how flat your plywood door stock is, you may want to consider installing roller friction catches in the cabinets to pull the doors tight when closed. However, the spring-loaded hinges will accomplish this purpose so long as the plywood door panels are sufficiently flat.*

PHOTO V: Drill holes between the cabinet compartments for running the necessary wires to power and connect your electronic equipment.

40 Install the pulls on the doors.

41 Insert the adjustable shelf pins and shelves, install your audio-visual components, and clip the fabric panels into their openings.

Index

Index of Projects